The Living Proof

A 31-DAY DEVOTIONAL
ON THE POWER OF YOUR WORDS

BY

stephanie d. moore

Published by
Moore Marketing and Communications
Oklahoma City, Oklahoma
www.StephanieDMoore.com

• Bulk copies or group sales of this book are available by contacting moore@stephaniedmoore.com or by calling (405) 306-9833.

FIRST EDITION PRINTED MAY 2019
Printed in USA

Moore, Stephanie D.
The Living Proof
First Edition.

Issued also as an ebook.

ISBN: 978-1-7337459-1-8

The Living Proof

Dedicated to My Grandmother,
Bertha M. Bradley

"Rejoice evermore.
Pray without ceasing.
In every thing give thanks:
for this is the will of God in Christ Jesus
concerning you."

I Thessalonians 5:16-18

Words Create, Destroy, & Echo

"Let the words of my mouth and the meditation of my heart
be acceptable in Your sight,
O Lord, my rock and my Redeemer."

Psalm 19:14

The Word of God shares that the power of life and death are in the tongue. Words create, destroy and echo. They can move a mountain of indifference or they can create a chasm of separation. Scripture affirms that it isn't what goes in the mouth of a man that defiles them, but what comes out that matters most. Our words can either bring peace or they can bring anguish. Faith comes by hearing - hearing the Word of God. And while, our attempt at righteousness maybe a filthy rag, we can speak with intention and bless the lives of those we love. This devotional is named for my grandmother. She lived a life that was honorable before God and I saw the promises of God exemplified through her. She was The Living Proof of what a life with God looks like. On her death bed she told me to never stop praying. This devotional will take a closer look at how many of the greats in the Bible used words to create, destroy, love and give God praise.

Testify

"Let the redeemed of the Lord say so,
whom he has redeemed from the hand of the enemy"
Psalm 107:2

In Context

The Lord is good and his mercy lasts forever. When we mess up and get in trouble, we can ask God for help. God will hear us and save us through the power of his Word. When God helps us, we are to give him praise so that he will receive the glory he deserves. Let us declare his goodness with gratitude! We see his miracles every day in the world that surrounds us. He blesses the earth. He punishes the high and mighty and adopts the poor. The righteous rejoice and sin shuts her mouth. A wise man witnesses this and understands the unending love of the Lord.

Life and Death

You can ruin your life with the words that you speak. I know. I have lost lifelong friends, business opportunities, familial relationships and more as a result. We must be careful of what we say... slow to speak and eager to understand. When your enemies rise up in multitudes to speak against you, pray for them and allow God to guide you. It will be difficult but stand in faith beneath the shadow of his wings and watch what you say. Give God the praise because he is faithful and he will never let you down.

"Through God we shall do valiantly: for he it is that shall tread down our enemies."
Psalm 108:13

In Context

David opens this chapter by telling God his heart is fixed. He's going to give God glory and praise for what God is going to do in his life. While David feels surrounded by enemies, he begins to speak the victory over them. He speaks life over his situation and proclaims that God will fight his battle and produce victory.

Final Notes

It is easy for us to get angry over unfair situations. We must admit that sometimes we cause those situations through poor decision-making. People can also be fickle and relationships have a natural ebb and flow of good times and bad. But, God is consistent. He sees the end from the beginning and nothing we experience is a surprise. He is trustworthy and will fight all of our battles if we let him. We must learn to speak life over our situations and turn them over to Jesus. Victory belongs to his children.

PRAYER

Most Gracious and Heavenly Father,

Let your words settle in our heart and direct our every step. Lord, suture our lips when we should be quiet, be still and just listen. Set a guard over our mouths and keep watch over the door of our lips. Help us to have ears of understanding and eyes to see as you do. Lord, victory, honor and glory belong to you. Let the redeemed of the Lord say so and help us to give you praise every day that we have breath. Thank you for our lives, your mercy and your grace. Help us to be the Living Proof that your Word never fails.

In Jesus Name, Amen.

Love

"Then she said, Let me find favor in thy sight, my lord;
for that thou hast comforted me and for that thou hast
spoken friendly unto thine handmaid, though I be not like
unto one of thine handmaidens."
Ruth 2:12

In Context

Ruth was daughter-in-law to a widow named Naomi.
Ruth's husband, had recently passed away. She
followed her mother-in-law home and left her own
family to take care of the older woman. Upon return
to Naomi's hometown, Ruth went out to find food for
she and Naomi. She went to a relative's field to get
any scraps of harvest she could muster. She was
from out of town and everyone recognized her as
Naomi's daughter-in-law. One day the owner of the
field saw her working hard and acknowledged her. He
told her how he admired her love for his relative and
that it was obvious she trusted God. He invited her to
dinner and allowed her to reap the harvest with his
handmaidens for the rest of the season. She thanked
him for his graciousness and returned home to share
the good news with her mother-in-law.

Loving Others

Loving others through our actions will unquestionably
get attention. Boaz, the owner of the field, took the
time to acknowledge his gratitude for her love and
care of his relative by sharing his thoughts with Ruth
directly. You never know who is watching you. After a
long day's work in a foreign land, picking up the scraps,
this acknowledgment went a long way with Ruth. I
am sure it meant the world to her to be noticed and

appreciated.

"And Jonathan spoke well of David to Saul his father and said to him, "Let not the king sin against his servant David, because he has not sinned against you, and because his deeds have brought good to you. For he took his life in his hand and he struck down the Philistine, and the Lord worked a great salvation for all Israel. You saw it, and rejoiced. Why then will you sin against innocent blood by killing David without cause?"
I Samuel 19:4

In Context

Saul was very jealous of his servant David. David was admired by the community and a valiant warrior. Saul wanted David dead and he devised a plan to kill him. But, his son Jonathan was great friends with David and did his best to defend him before his father. He also warned David of the impending danger. Because Jonathan reasoned with Saul, his father subdued his anger and promised not to kill David. But, once Jonathon brought David to see his father, the king's anger was rekindled. He lunged his spear at David and attempted to kill him. David escaped. His wife (Saul's daughter) protected him by disguising a dummy in her bed and telling the king's servants that David was sick, while David secretly left to a place of safety. He went to live in Naioth with Samuel, a prophet. Saul found out where he was hiding and sent messengers. The messengers began to prophesy with Samuel upon arrival. Saul sent an additional two group of messengers and they began to prophesy (rather than give Saul's message to Samuel). Saul himself came to find David. As he got closer to the Naioth, he too began prophesying. In fact, he stripped off his clothing and lay on the ground before Samuel and prophesied all day and night.

Final Notes

Your words can encourage, protect and most importantly, love. Your intentions are empowered by the use of your words. Boaz desired to comfort and express gratitude, while Jonathon desired to protect. Those that sought David were instructed to take David, but instead were overcome by the Spirit of God and began to pronounce blessings through prophesy. Even the very man that desired to kill him began to prophesy as he got closer and closer to a group of people speaking a blessing into the atmosphere. Our words are containers that carry our love to the intended recipient in a way that clearly expresses we care.

PRAYER

Most Gracious and Heavenly Father,

Thank you for the gift of spoken word. Help us to love others through our use of words. Help us to protect, empower, comfort, encourage and bless. Lord, please forgive us when we use our words to tear down, hurt and belittle others. Help us to be wise. Help us to think before we speak. Help us to create opportunities for others to love through their use of words and help us to become better and more loving communicators. Like apples of gold in settings of silver is a word spoken in right circumstances.

In Jesus Name, Amen.

Do the Work

"Now when Ezra had prayed, and when he had confessed, weeping and casting himself down before the house of God, there assembled unto him out of Israel a very great congregation of men and women and children: for the people wept very sore."

Ezra 10:1

In Context

Ezra realized that there was a great sin and horrible destiny in store for his people if they stayed on their current course. So, he prayed with his whole heart and from a place of true sincerity. As he prayed, the people began to join him, as they too, realized they were headed for destruction. Israel had taken wives that were forbidden by God based on their culture and ritualistic ways. The son of Jehiel responded to the outcry by sharing that even though they sinned, there was still hope for Israel. The people agreed that it was time to rid themselves of the foreign wives and offspring created by their forbidden unions. But they knew it would be a great work and take time. Together, their leadership looked at the problem and created a solution.

Praying for a Solution

Our words are very powerful. They matter to God and they matter to those around us. We often take missteps that result in poor decisions that can send us in a spiral of destruction. But, if we hold fast to the truth and confess our sins to God, we still have hope. Not only will he forgive us, he will give us a plan that can't fail.

"And I said unto the nobles, and to the rulers, and to the rest of the people, the work is great and large, and we are separated upon the wall, one far from another. In what place therefore ye hear the sound of the trumpet, resort ye thither unto us: our God shall fight for us."
Nehemiah 4:19-20

In Context

Nehemiah and the Jews were appointed a special task to rebuild the walls of Jerusalem. As they began their work, their enemies mocked their capability. After hearing what was being said, he and his team prayed to God to give Sanballat and Tobiah (their enemies) a boomerang of what they intended to do to the Jews and their work. When their enemies heard how quickly and beautifully the repairs were coming, in anger, Sanballat and Tabiah were determined to destroy them and assured many others that Nehemiah and his team would never see them coming. In response, Nehemiah and his team prayed again, this time while also keeping an eye out for the enemy. Some of the Jews were afraid and felt surrounded. Nehemiah told the Jews, "Do not be afraid of them, remember the Lord which is great and terrible, and fight for your brethren, your sons, your daughters, your wives and your houses." Then, from that day forward, they split up their workload – half work, half defense, some with tools in one hand, weapons in the other.

Final Notes

Your prayers can help you accomplish your goals. They can open the door to forgiveness. They can call for a response from God for strategic help. They can be a defense when the enemy is trying to destroy you. Your words are clear and concise gateways for work to be completed and can deploy the ultimate defense mechanism, God himself. Speak life that it may be well with you and your children.

PRAYER

Most Gracious and Heavenly Father,

You are a way maker, a deliverer, a mighty conqueror and a strong tower in the day of trouble. We thank you and honor you. Lord, teach us to do the work with our words to utilize prayer as a pathway to justice and peace; to speak what we believe and know about you and your faithfulness, to fall down on our faces and beg your forgiveness when we know we are wrong, and to use our words to forgive others that have wronged us. Lord help us to speak life, love and mature thoughts. Help us to be perfect conduits of your message for your people at the right time.

In Jesus Name, Amen.

Imitate Me

"So you must be careful to do everything they tell you.
But do not do what they do,
for they do not practice what they preach."
Matthew 23:3

In Context

Jesus began teaching about hypocrisy in the
temple. How those who teach the law are often not
performing what they teach. He reminds them that
they have one father, God and one teacher, himself.
He also explains that the greatest among them
serve with humility. He then shares seven warnings to
teachers of the law: Do not block the way into heaven
with heavy words you won't live up to; do not chase
a soul only to corrupt it; understand the power of
your words when swearing; do not put more weight
on the details of worship yet ignore justice, mercy and
faithfulness; don't be so quick to clean the outside
of a cup but leaving the filth inside – clean the inside
first; don't be a hypocrite – be what you teach; and
don't hurt those sent to prophesy the Word of God.
He ended his message with a solemn promise, 'You
will not see me again until you say, Blessed is he
comes in the name of the Lord.'

Actions Speak Louder than Words

When our words and actions don't align we can really
hinder the gospel of Jesus Christ. Jesus enters the
temple with one universal message - be what you
say you are. He outlines their hypocrisy to the letter
and shares an impending doom for those that don't
take notice.

"Out of the same mouth come praise and cursing.
My brothers and sisters, this should not be."
James 3:10

In Context

Teaching isn't for everyone because you will be judged
more strictly... and we all make mistakes. Our mouths
are powerful because words create and destroy. We
often praise God and curse but this isn't right. Those
wise and understanding will be reflected in good
life and their deeds will be done in humility. Where
you have envy and selfish ambition, there you find
disorder and every evil practice. Peacemakers who
sow in peace reap a harvest of righteousness.

Final Notes

Your walk is just as important as your talk. Sometimes
the best speaking comes from your actions. But if
you do speak, as a teacher or simply an ambassador
of Jesus Christ, remember that people are watching
and paying attention. Blessing and cursing should
not flow from the same place. Also, we must walk in
humility.

PRAYER

Most Gracious and Heavenly Father,

We thank you for the precious gift of correction. We
can't always see ourselves the way you do, and we
need a helpful hand to gently lead us the right way.
Lord, suture our lips and help us to just be quiet, be
still and just listen when it is right. Help us to create
according to your will when we speak. Help us to walk
what we say. Help us to lead in heavenly direction,
making sure the inside is just as clean as the outside
looks. Please forgive us of our sins. Thank you for your
love, your mercy and your grace.

In Jesus Name, Amen.

SPEAK LIFE   I abide in God, and his Words within me.

Shadows

"I have put My words in your mouth and have covered you with the shadow of My hand, to establish the heavens, to found the earth, and to say to Zion, 'You are My people."
Isaiah 51:16

In Context

God speaks to his children. I am going to rescue you from your enemies. I will shine a light on your path, those that seek me. I comfort you and protect you, the people you fear are simply throwing tantrums. I was angry at you and gave you a cup of rage that had you drunk and alone in the streets of bitterness. No one came to help. No one offered help. You were forced to submit beneath your enemies as they trampled all over you... and used you as their doormat. But I have heard your cries and it is their turn to drink my wrath.

Beneath the Shadow of His Wings

Sometimes, God allows us to suffer through the storm. We may have brought the storm on ourselves through selfish action or indifference to God's command. Nonetheless, his anger is but for a moment and his love is for a lifetime. The enemies we see today, we won't see anymore. We have no need to fear, because even when we make mistakes, God is right there to protect us and vengeance belongs to him.

"For You have been a defense for the helpless, A defense for the needy in his distress, A refuge from the storm, a shade from the heat; For the breath of the ruthless Is like a

rain storm against a wall. Like heat in drought, You subdue
the uproar of aliens; Like heat by the shadow of a cloud,
the song of the ruthless is silenced."
Isaiah 25:4-5

In Context

I celebrate and praise you, you are my God. You have
destroyed my enemies and protected the poor. On
this mountain, we celebrate God's victory over death.
He will wipe our tears away and restore our name.
We will shout and sing praise to God because we
waited for him. We waited, he showed up and saved
us! Our enemies pride will pull them under. Their
protection slowly slipping away into nothingness.

Final Notes

Storms may come but we can still give God the
praise. In our patience and faith, we will see victory.
He will fight every battle for us. As we speak
life, asking for forgiveness, giving him praise and
confessing our faith we can stand confident in
knowing help is on the way. Embrace faith over fear.

PRAYER
Most Gracious and Heavenly Father,

Please forgive us of our sins.
Help us to be everything you have created us to
be. Help us to speak confidently, positively and
unwaveringly of our faith in you and your protection.
Help us to speak words of victory in our greatest
moments of fear. Help us to speak of the qualities that
rest in patient victory. Thank you Lord for fighting our
battles and allowing us the peace of resting beneath
the shadow of your wings, amid the chaos that
unwittingly tries to destroy us.
We cast our cares upon you.

In Jesus Name, Amen.

SPEAK LIFE I believe God and it is counted as righteousness.

Becoming

> "I said, 'I have been banished from your sight; yet I will look
> again toward your holy temple.'"
> Jonah 2:4

In Context

God gave Jonah a specific assignment. But Jonah
didn't want to do it. Instead he ran. As a result, Jonah
found himself inside the belly of a whale deep in the
bottom of the sea. In this chapter, he cries out to God,
begging for forgiveness and acknowledging his wrong.
God forgave Jonah and the whale spit him up on dry
ground.

Becoming

Sometimes in order to become what God has
designed us to be, we must see what is on the other
side. Discomfort, pain, shame and sadness all come
to mind when I consider going against the will of God.
But God. Prayer changes things. When we go left and
God tells us to go right, we can stand in faith that God
will forgive us if we ask and he will course correct us.
Words have the power of forgiveness and the power
of blessing. Our words can also elevate us and bring
us to a place that is exceedingly, abundantly, more
than we can ask or imagine.

> "Jabez cried out to the God of Israel, "Oh, that you would
> bless me and enlarge my territory! Let your hand be with
> me and keep me from harm so that I will be free from
> pain." And God granted his request."
> I Chronicles 4:10

In Context

There are several chapters in the Bible in which God gives great detail. If you aren't paying attention when God gives descriptive detail (I am guilty), you will miss this verse in your daily reading. As 1 Chronicles 4 details the lineage of Judah, it pauses and acknowledges the statement of Jabez, then goes right back to sharing details of the lineage. Jabez asks God to bless, add and protect him – and God granted his request.

Final Notes

Our words have tremendous power and God is listening. **You will become what you say.** He hears every utterance. Words are containers of power that echo throughout time. We should be very careful how we use them. God has intentionally sprinkled moments throughout the Bible with characters that seem to be ordinary people whose words have impressed God. From Rahab to Jabez, to Ruth to Jonah. Prayer is our direct line and connection to God. God is listening – he hears every word we say. The Bible also gives us great examples of what to say and how to say it. It is our responsibility to share the gospel with our family and those we encounter. From our hearts to God's ears, we must weigh what we think, say and believe – we do have an audience of One and he has the power to change our lives dramatically.

PRAYER

Most Gracious and Heavenly Father,

We call upon heaven and declare that we are blessed. We are blessed in the city and we are blessed in the field, we are blessed everywhere we go. We are the head and not the tail, above and not beneath. We are blessed. Lord, as we pray for blessings, we know that we often speak what should not be spoken. Good and bad should not come from the same place. Help us as we experience hardship, anger, disappointment and pain. Help us Lord, in those moments to suture our lips, be still, be quiet and just listen to what you have to say. Help us Lord, to ponder our thoughts and speak with wisdom. Lord, teach us to pray according to your will and heal our hearts. Strengthen us for the battle that lies ahead and prepare us for the destiny you have designed. When we fall short, help us to pray for forgiveness and the strength to forgive others. Help us to intercede on behalf of our friends, family and those in need. Lord, give us the power to pray for right motives, a right foundation based upon your Word, a right spirit filled with compassion and love... and most of all, a true and devoted relationship with you. Help us to seek your face and not your hand in our moments of greatest need. Lord, help us to become all that you created us to be.

In Jesus Name, Amen.

Hatred

"Hatred stirs up conflict, but love covers over all wrongs."
Proverbs 10:12

In Context

Proverbs 10 shares many truths about the intentions, purpose and result of what we say. From the mouth of the righteous comes the fruit of wisdom, but a perverse tongue will be silenced. Wisdom is found on the lips of the discerning, but a rod is for the back of one who has no sense. Whoever conceals hatred with lying lips and spreads slander is a fool. Sin is not ended by multiplying words, but the prudent hold their tongues. A fool finds pleasure in wicked schemes, but a person of understanding delights in wisdom.

Conflict & Words

We can cause so much pain with our words. They can create havoc within our families, destroy friendships and ruin the best of relationships. But if we speak, we must do so with wisdom and discernment. After it is all said and done (after the chaos), the righteous will remain standing. Long life is a gift to those that fear the Lord, but the years of the wicked are cut short. God's way will protect us, but it ends poorly for those who do evil.

"Then Amnon hated her with a very great hatred; for the hatred with which he hated her was greater than the love with which he had loved her. And Amnon said to her,
"Get up, go away!"
2 Samuel 2:15

In Context

Tamar was a beautiful virgin. Her half-brother, Amnon fell in love with her. His uncle and advisor told him to ask his father to send her to make him a meal because he was ill. Her father ordered her to go and she baked Amnon a loaf of bread. When she was ready to serve, he ordered everyone out of his room and raped her. She begged him not to, but he did it anyway. Afterward, he kicked her out. She again, begged him not to, but he did it anyway. Their brother, Absalom was furious, but he never said a word to Amnon good or bad. Two years pass, and Absalom invites his father and brothers to a feast. King David insisted he could not attend but reluctantly allowed Amnon to go. At the feast, Absalom's servants murder Amnon at his instruction. Absalom flees. David got word that Absalom murdered all his brothers, but David's brother and Amnon's adviser assured him it was only Amnon. King David mourned Amnon and missed Absalom.

Final Notes

The power of life and death are in the tongue. Poor advice, ignoring the warnings, and anger can create pathways of destruction. God warns us that ungodly behavior, lies, and making selfish choices can all lead to a very poor end.

PRAYER

Most Gracious and Heavenly Father,

Thank you for your whisper of confident grace, mercy and love. Help us to speak words of wisdom during conflict. Help us to suture our lips, be still and be quiet when we are unsure of what to say or should say nothing at all. Help us to see past our offender to the cross of forgiveness. Help us to say less, think more and obtain greater understanding. Lord, we know that the mouth of the righteous utters wisdom, and their tongues speak what is right. Help us to speak what is right, what is good and what is truthful. We honor you, praise you, and uplift your holy and righteous name.

In Jesus Name, Amen.

Blessing

"But blessed is the one who trusts in the Lord, whose confidence is in him. They will be like a tree planted by the water that sends out its roots by the stream. It does not fear when heat comes; its leaves are always green. It has no worries in a year of drought and never fails to bear fruit."
Jeremiah 17:7-8

In Context

God says, "Judah's sin is engraved in stone. Their sin will cause them to lose their inheritance and make them slaves to their enemies. I will enslave you to your enemies in a land you do not know. Cursed is the one who trusts in man. But blessed is the one who trusts in the Lord, whose confidence is in him. The heart is deceitful above all things and beyond cure. Who can understand it? I search the heart and examine the mind, to reward each person according to their conduct, according to what their deeds deserve." Jeremiah responds, "Lord, you are the hope of Israel, all who forsake you will be ashamed. Heal me and I will be healed; save me and I will be saved, for you are the one I praise. Let my persecutors be put to shame, but keep me from shame; let them be terrified, but keep me from terror. Bring on them the day of disaster; destroy them with double destruction." God says, "But if you do not obey me to keep the Sabbath day holy by not carrying any load as you come through the gates of Jerusalem on the Sabbath day, then I will kindle an unquenchable fire in the gates of Jerusalem that will consume her fortresses."

The Blessing and The Curse

God is very clear about what he expects and requires. He does not hide his intent. We don't always know how he will work but we know that God will perform everything he promised. He is faithful. Our responsibility lies in how we respond to God and what he shares will produce the blessing or the curse. We are to honor him with words and actions. We are to respect the Sabbath and trust only him. It's really very simple in that we are not overrun with sin, God gives us a way to escape sin every time. We must obey his will and bless others. If not, his promises of the curse will come to pass and it cannot surprise us. We must repent and do his will.

"Blessed is the one who does not walk in step with the wicked or stand in the way that sinners take or sit in the company of mockers, but whose delight is in the law of the Lord, and who meditates on his law, day and night."
Psalm 1:1-2

In Context

Blessed are those who delight in the law of the Lord and who meditate on it day and night. They will yield fruit in their due season. But the wicked will blow away with the wind. The Lord watches over the way of the righteous, but the way of the wicked leads to destruction.

Final Notes

There is a vast difference between the blessing and the curse. We have the choice to live our lives the way we see fit, but God gives us clear instruction on how to be blessed and how to be cursed.

PRAYER

Most Gracious and Heavenly Father,

Lord, you have given us everything we need. You are a strong tower and a very present help in the time of trouble. While we can choose to live the way we desire, help us to hear your voice, heed your warnings and to appreciate your grace. You are our rock and shield. We are the apple of your eye. Forgive us of our sins and help us to forgive those that hurt us with intention. Lord, help us to be your hands and feet in this earth. Give us the voice of truth and suture our lips when words of resentment or anger arise. Thank you for the blessing of your words to us. Thank you for the gift of prayer and intimacy with you. Thank you for being our Father and endowing us with the Holy Spirit. Thank you for keeping us in the middle of a storm. Please grant us specific wisdom for our situations. Order our steps. Measure our hearts. Help us to walk in truth. Help us to exchange our worry for an unquenchable thirst for you that develops an anchored trust.

In Jesus Name, Amen.

David:
Touch Not My Anointed

"And David said to him, "Your blood be upon your head; your own mouth has testified against you, saying, "I have slain the Lord's anointed." 2 Samuel 1:16

In Context

After Saul died, a young Amalekite man shared the news with David's camp. David asked how he knew of Saul and Jonathan's death. The young man told him Saul called for him from the battlefield after receiving a fatal wound. He asked the young man to finish the job by standing on top of him, therefore pushing him further down upon his spear and killing him. The young man obliged and afterward took his crown and bracelet. These he presented to David. Immediately, David summoned one of his men to kill the young man. As the young man lay dying, David said to him, "Your blood be upon your head; your own mouth has testified against you, saying, "I have slain the Lord's anointed." David mourned the death of Saul and David, telling no one to spread the word and teaching young children how to use the bow. He also called them lovely and testified that Jonathon's love was great... greater than the love of any woman.

The Honor of Serving God

"Vengeance is mine," says the Lord, "I will repay." As a child of God, we are called to a higher level of conduct and response. While we are often still attacked by our enemies, we are to turn the other cheek and let God avenge those that try to destroy us. It's true that sometimes our anger can get the best of us. We may strike back because the pain ran deeper than we expected. At other times, we may resort to isolation and unforgiveness. But, as the hands and feet of Jesus, we are called to speak, act and think a different way. We all sin. It is the reason we sin that requires we forgive. When people sin, the reasoning isn't as bad as the vehicle chosen to deliver the desired results. A single mom wishing to feed her family, choosing sin as a means to gain income... is bad. However, the reason she is sinning is not. We must be patient, listen and pray for those that despitefully use us or try their best to abuse us. Remember, God is in control.

"And he said unto his men, The Lord forbid that I should do this thing unto my master, the Lord's anointed, to stretch forth mine hand against him, seeing he is the anointed of the Lord."
I Samuel 24:6

In Context

After pursuing the Philistines in battle, Saul and three thousand of his men looked for David. Saul wanted to kill him. During their journey, they rested in a cave. The very cave they chose to rest in also held David and his men. David's men tried to convince him to kill Saul in his sleep. They told him that God delivered his enemy into his hand. David got up and cut off a portion of Saul's robe. David felt guilty. He knew he should not have cut Saul's robe. It was a threat. David admitted he was wrong and that God would not have wanted him to do that. In that way, he kept his men from attacking Saul. Saul soon awakened and left the cave, with David coming out afterward. David called out to him and bowed before him. He shared that he could have harmed Saul, that his men encouraged him to do so. But, that he showed mercy and respect for God's anointed. He showed Saul the robe in his hand to reflect that there was neither evil or transgression in his hand. Then he shared, the Lord judge between me and you: and avenge me for you, but my hand shall not touch you. Saul heard David and began to cry. He told him, you are more righteous than me because you have been good to me and I have been evil to you. He then asked David to swear not to destroy his seed after he is gone. David promised not to, and they departed ways.

Final Notes

We are honor God's people. It is an honor and responsibility to uphold them in high regard. Whether they treat you the way you are supposed to be treated or not, you are not to touch them for they are God's anointed. In the same way, God will avenge those that do their best to hurt you because you serve him.

PRAYER

Most Gracious and Heavenly Father,

Lord, thank you for showing us the example of David. Help us to honor those that serve you with our hearts, minds, actions and words. Help us to lift them up, even when they try to tear us down. Help us to shine a bright light on your work in our lives by changing how we respond to conflict. Lord, we know that those that wait on you shall renew their strength. We are waiting on you to avenge us, we will not lash out or speak negatively. Instead, we will go into our secret place, our prayer closet and turn it over to you. Lord, you are our rock, our shield and our exceeding great reward. We call those things that are not as though they already are. We are the head and not the tail. We are above and not beneath. We are the lenders and not the borrowers. We are your children and we bless your holy and righteous name.

In Jesus Name, Amen.

Ruth:
Going to Work

"One day, Ruth, the Moabite foreigner, said to Naomi, "I'm going to work; I'm going out to glean among the sheaves, following after some harvester who will treat me kindly."
Ruth 2:2

In Context

Ruth was daughter-in-law to Naomi. She clung to Naomi at their toughest time. They were poor and leaving their home to go to Naomi's homeland. Ruth refused to leave her mother-in-law and determined herself to worship Naomi's God. She promised Naomi that nothing but death would keep them apart. Upon arrival, Naomi shared she had a relative that was wealthy with a farm. Ruth decided to go to his farm and see if one of the workers would be kind enough to allow her to pick up the scraps. A little while after she began working Boaz came out and inquired about her. The harvesters shared that she asked permission to collect their scraps and spoke of how hard she works. Boaz spoke to Ruth: "Don't go to another field, always come here and follow my young women. Watch where they go and follow them. Ruth fell to her knees in gratitude and thanked him. He told her that he heard about her devotion to Naomi and her trust in God. He invited her to rest and have lunch. After lunch, he told his servants to leave her extra grain on the ground and to make it easy for her. She returned home and told Naomi of the blessing they received at the hands of Boaz. Naomi blessed God and testified, "He still loves us in bad times and good!"

The Lord of Increase

God is omniscient. He is aware of your current situation and he is going to bless you as long as you continue to trust him and work hard. God is sending people that will be good to you. Just trust and believe.

"If you say so, I'll do it, just as you've told me."
Ruth 3:5

In Context

Naomi felt it was time to make her daughter a good home. She told Ruth to visit Boaz on a great day of celebration and to wait until he is content with food and drink. Then Ruth was to follow Boaz and sleep at his feet (signifying she was available for marriage). She told her mother in law she would do as instructed. She followed her directions to the letter. Boaz awoke to find Ruth at his feet. He felt honored at her invitation to be her husband because she was beautiful and had a good reputation. He promised to ensure he could marry her because there was another man that technically had the right and he wanted his permission. As Ruth prepared to leave his presence early in the morning, he provided her with six measures of barley. She went home and told her mother-in-law all about it. She assured Ruth that Boaz would do what he promised and quickly.

Final Notes

The Lord sees your beauty and the way you have been representing his kingdom before the world. He sees your heart and has heard your call. He, just like Boaz is honored to call you his own. He will redeem you and make you his. You will find rest with him and he will right his name on your heart.

PRAYER

Most Gracious and Heavenly Father,

Lord Jesus, help us to see you and hear from you in hard times. Help us to work hard and be productive. Help us to see you in the midst of the storm. Help us to recognize you as our Boaz, our kinsman redeemer. Lord Jesus, protect us from the enemy. Help us to raise up holy hands, to offer up words of prayer, to speak your truth and sing your praise. Help us to strengthen our faith and help us to believe every promise. Help us to be strong Lord.

In Jesus Name, Amen.

Rahab:
God is With You

"Before the spies lay down for the night, she went up on the roof and said to them, "I know that the LORD has given you this land and that a great fear of you has fallen on us, so that all who live in this country are melting in fear because of you."
Joshua 2:8-9

In Context

Joshua sent two men to spy out the land of Jericho. Rahab was a prostitute living in Jericho. The men went straight to Rahab's house. The king heard the men were in town to spy out the land and sent his servants to retrieve the men. However, when they arrived at Rahab's house, she lied and told them the men left before the city gate closed. She then told the men to hide on her roof. They later escaped into the hills at Rahab's suggestion and avoided capture. But, before the men left, Rahab shared how her entire community feared them because God was with them. She asked that when the men returned to take the city, they spare her and the life of her family. The men agreed, saying a "life for a life" because she saved their lives. They then gave her specific instructions on how to ensure she and her family would not be harmed when they came to take the city. She responded, "Let it be as you say."

God is With You

When we walk with God, our life will have evidence. We will bear fruit that remains. That means that what we do with God as our head, will stand for eternity.

His purpose for our lives will always allow us to help others. His purpose for our lives will always have provision, protection and divine direction. Rahab's purpose was to protect the men of God, in doing so, she saved her own life. Her words empowered her...

"Then the Lord said to Joshua,
"See, I have delivered Jericho into your hands,
along with its king and its fighting men."
Joshua 6:2

In Context

The Lord told Joshua that they would win the battle at Jericho, but they had very detailed instructions. Each of the men had to be circumcised. Joshua was to pull one young man from each tribe to follow the priests. They had to follow from a specific distance. They also had to cross the Jordan Sea. The priests would enter the water first. It was the time of flooding so the water within the sea was surging. But the moment the priests put their foot in the water, it stopped flowing to and out. In fact, the land they stood on became dry ground and the army of the Lord was able to cross on dry ground. God told Joshua to have one man from each tribe go into the Jordan and get a rock. The rocks would serve as a memorial for generations to come about their victory with God. The rocks were assembled by Joshua near their camp. They were to enter into the promised land and march around the gated city in a specific formation. God told them, "March around the city once with all the armed men. Do this for six days. Have seven priests carry trumpets of rams' horns in front of the ark. On the seventh day, march around the city seven times, with the priests blowing the trumpets. When you hear them sound a long blast on the trumpets, have the whole army give a loud shout; then the wall of the city will collapse and the army will go up, everyone straight in." Rahab and her family did exactly what was instructed and were saved.

Final Notes

Obedience and faithful confession go hand-in-hand. God gave Rahab and Joshua detailed instruction on how to win the fight. We must have faith. We must believe and trust God, no matter what it looks like, we must believe.

PRAYER
Most Gracious and Heavenly Father,

Lord, I know that you are for us. You are helping us to travel into our promised land on dry ground. Lord, you faithfully direct our path and make it straight. Help us to see you in every situation. Help us to do your will. Help us to speak your words. Help us to see that no matter our situation, you have us in the palm of your hand.

In Jesus Name, Amen.

Jacob:
Not Unless You Bless Me

"So Jacob was left alone, and a man wrestled with him till daybreak. When the man saw that he could not overpower him, he touched the socket of Jacob's hip so that his hip was wrenched as he wrestled with the man. Then the man said, "Let me go, for it is daybreak." But Jacob replied, "I will not let you go unless you bless me." The man asked him, "What is your name?" "Jacob," he answered. Then the man said, "Your name will no longer be Jacob, but Israel, because you have struggled with God and with humans and have overcome."
Genesis 32:24-28

In Context

Jacob was the youngest son of Isaac. He tricked his father into giving him his brother Esau's blessing then ran in fear of his life. The blessing anointed him to become father to the 12 tribes of Israel and marry two of his mother's nieces. But, when he got to Nahor, his father-in-law tricked him and took advantage of his hard work. After 20 years, God spoke to Jacob and told him to return home. He did what God asked but sent messengers ahead to share the news with his estranged brother. On his journey home, he met a man (the angel of God) and wrestled with him until daybreak. The man asked him to let him go, but Jacob refused to let go until he blessed him. The man touched his hip and knocked it out of socket. Then Jacob asked him his name. The man instead gave Jacob the new name of Israel because he struggled with God and man and overcame.

Struggling with God and Man

We can make poor decisions that put us in a bad light with God and man. We will suffer for a little while, but God promises his anger is but for a moment, his favor for a lifetime. This too shall pass. There is also great power in the blessing. Jacob was blessed because he received Isaac's blessing. He also refused to let the man go until he blessed him as well. Speak life that it may be well with you and your children.

"The Lord bless you and keep you; the Lord make his face shine on you and be gracious to you; the Lord turn his face toward you and give you peace."
Numbers 6:24-26

In Context

God has given detailed destruction on how to remain pure in Numbers 5. In Numbers 6, he shares how to dedicate yourself properly in worship. From what you drink, to how you groom, to what you can allow in your atmosphere – this book outlines very specific instruction on how to worship as a Nazirite. Finally, he teaches Moses how to bless the Israelites.

Final Notes

We can be blessed or cursed. The power of life and death is in our tongue. While no weapon formed against you shall prosper, your words can cause a snare that will have you wrestling with God and man. Whatever you do, don't doubt God. Consecrate yourself, worship, repent and trust him.
He will never fail.

PRAYER

Most Gracious and Heavenly Father,

Thank you for the power of your Word. Thank you for

forgiveness, mercy and grace. Thank you for seeing the end before the beginning. We are so blessed! Your grace is sufficient for in our weakness is your strength made perfect. When we fall, we can get back up. When we pray, we can be confident that you hear us and will answer. Lord, give us strategic wisdom that is timely and relevant in our place of great need.
Help us to be everything you created us to be.
Forgive us and restore us.

In Jesus Name, Amen.

Joseph:
They Meant It for Evil

"Here comes that dreamer!" they said to each other.
"Come now, let's kill him and throw him into one of these
cisterns and say that a ferocious animal devoured him.
Then we'll see what comes of his dreams."
Genesis 37:19-20

In Context

Joseph was seventeen and his father Jacob's
favorite son. Jacob made Joseph a beautiful coat
of many colors. His father often kept him at home
while his brothers worked in the field. Joseph would
go and see what they were doing and how they
were doing in the field and report back to his father...
sometimes telling on them. On two occasions, Joseph
had dreams that signified he would be the greatest in
the family and that the remainder of his family would
one day bow down to him. This angered his brothers
and troubled his father's thoughts. After having these
dreams, his father asked him to once again check
on his brothers. They were not where they were
supposed to be. A local man directed him to where he
could find them. Once they saw Joseph coming, they
plotted to kill him. One of the older brothers, insisted
killing him was not the answer. He suggested throwing
him in a cistern for a while with the intent of going
to get him later. When a band of Ishmaelites rode
by, his brothers sold him into slavery for 20 pieces
of silver. When Reuben, the older brother went to
retrieve Joseph, he saw that he was no longer in the
cistern. Panic-stricken, he went to the other brothers
and asked about him. They grabbed Joseph's coat of
many colors and drenched it in goat's blood. They took

the coat back to their father, asking if he recognized the coat. His father was distraught and mourned Joseph for a long time. Joseph was then sold to Potiphar (a high-ranking official in Pharaoh's house) in Egypt.

Beyond a Dream

We all want to one day look back on our lives and thank God for the impact he has allowed us to make. Somewhere, deep in our hearts, we know we were created for greatness. Some of us have dreams that seem impossible. No matter where we are in life or the pursuit of that dream, others can't envision what we do. God places a special gift inside of us to help us obtain that dream but we must believe in ourselves. This can be difficult when tough circumstances arise. We can begin to doubt what we know and believe. But God desires that we trust him and him alone. He will see us through. We may have seasons of pain, defeat, betrayal and misfires... but God is. His ways are not our ways and his thoughts are not our thoughts. He has a plan to uplift you, not destroy. Trust him and push through.

"But Joseph said to them, "Don't be afraid.
Am I in the place of God? You intended to harm me,
but God intended it for good to accomplish what is now
being done, the saving of many lives."
Genesis 50:19-20

In Context

Joseph suffered greatly while enslaved. Even when he provided excellent service, accusations and hard experiences would arise. Finally, after a long period of suffering, he was recognized by Pharaoh for his intelligence and ability to interpret dreams. By then, it was obvious to all that Joseph was anointed for greatness. He became second in command to

Pharaoh's kingdom in Egypt. A famine arose and the brothers that sold him into slavery traveled to Egypt where they heard there was food. This is when a painful reuniting took place between Joseph and the brothers that betrayed him. Joseph had to face an internal battle and choose between forgiveness and destruction. He wept and forgave. But, Joseph was able to see his father and little brother (who he loved and missed greatly) again. Soon, his father passed, blessing each of his sons and his grandsons (Joseph's sons) before his death. Afterward, Joseph's brothers were afraid of retaliation, but Joseph remained good to them throughout his reign. He told his brothers, God would tell them when to return home and to be sure and take his body with them when they go. After living 110 years, he passed away.

Final Notes

Life can seem unfair. Even when you see the promise of blessing and work hard to obtain it... you can still end up suffering in hardship. But, like Joseph, we must never doubt God and his intentions toward us. We must stand strong and stay in faith. Like Jacob, we have to watch what we say and what we believe. Joseph never repented of his dreams. He never took back his word... even when his father was troubled by the saying, he never took it back. He knew what God showed him was real and true. His confession was always yes and Amen to God's revelation of future success.

PRAYER

Most Gracious and Heavenly Father,

Thank you for allowing us to breathe another day. Thank you, we do not have the spirit of fear but that of a sound mind. Thank you for the provision, protection and direction. Thank you for wisdom and discernment. Lord, help us to remember, believe and obtain your promises in the Word. You promised that the water may come up to our necks, but not overtake us. You promised that we could exchange our heavy burdens for your light burden. You promised that we could cast our cares upon you because you care for us. While the road may seem too much to bear, help us to stand still and see the salvation of the Lord. Help us to let it go and allow you to do it. Help us to speak your Word. No weapon formed against us shall prosper. You will prepare a table before us in the presence of our enemies. Your angels are encamped around us in protection. Lord, forgive us and help us to forgive our enemies. Finally, Lord, help us to remember that we wrestle not against flesh and blood but principalities of evil. This battle is not ours, it belongs to you. As we delight ourselves in you, you are granting the desires of our hearts. We believe and confess.

In Jesus Name, Amen.

John:
There Will Be Joy

"Until now you have not asked for anything in my name. Ask and you will receive, and your joy will be complete."
John 16:24

In Context

Jesus is preparing us for rough times ahead. You will be thrown out of meetings and people will destroy you on purpose – thinking they are doing the will of God. But, its because they don't understand him. This is a warning, so you will be prepared. Jesus will provide the Holy Spirit to comfort you. He will identify sin as disbelief in Jesus, the source and provider of righteousness. Judgement comes from the evil rule that will end. The Holy Spirit will bring what Jesus gives to you. This made the disciples curious and full of wonder. Jesus explained that immense pain would come as the evil rejoice. But, it will turn around and your sadness will develop into gladness. In this way, the process will feel like childbirth. Pain and then joy. Jesus tells us to ask in His name and according to His will and whatever we ask for will be granted, so that we can have abundant joy. We are to pray to our Father in heaven, in whom we trust because of Jesus, and who loves us. While we will experience difficulties, we will also have the peace that God provides. Jesus has conquered this world.

Trust God, Embrace Peace and Love

In recent times, I faced immense difficulty in business. It was a season of distrust, betrayal and outright attack. However, God has allowed me to hear him through the Holy Spirit at every step of the way. This season is earmarked by transition. I realized, we can choose to elevate or fail. But, the choice is ours. The way we make choices must be led by God and not simply the desires of our hearts, but by also what will work best for us in this season. While, we face attacks, God is with us. Prayer is our most effective and proficient communication tool. If we pray in Jesus name and ask according to His will, all will be well.

"I have much to write to you, but I do not want to use paper and ink. Instead, I hope to visit you and talk with you face to face, so that our joy may be complete."
2 John 1:12

In Context

A letter written to the woman of God: Grace, mercy and peace from the Father and Son. I ask that we love, by walking in obedience to his command, which is to love one another. There are many that do not believe in Jesus Christ – beware of them that you do not be fooled by them and lose all that you have. Don't run ahead and stop preaching about Jesus Christ. Get your reward. While I have much to write, I hope to visit face-to-face and heart-to-heart.

Final Notes

We are to love our enemies. Even those we may think are trying to destroy us. In this way, we win the war against evil. Allow people to see the God in you, not the fight, the anger or the bitter response. Grow up, speak life, love and trust God. In the end, we win. Don't worry about it, pray about it. Joy comes in the morning.

PRAYER

Most Gracious and Heavenly Father,

Thank you for your abundant promises of peace, love and joy. While hard times must come, we know that in the end we win. Thank you for directing our paths and making them straight. Lord, on this day, we pray for a supernatural anointing of wisdom and discernment. We pray for peace that surpasses understanding. We pray that you encamp your angels around us in protection. We pray that we make choices that are pleasing in your sight. We pray for an abundance of your Holy Spirit, as we decrease and you increase. Open doors of favor and blessing, let your oil run fresh over us – anointing us for your work. Lord, as we walk in your light, love, and lavish presence help us to remember we are your ambassadors in the earth. Help us to suture our lips, be quiet and be still when we should listen. Help us to hear not only the words people speak but truly comprehend their meaning and purpose. Prepare us for the journey ahead and help us to work hard, pray without ceasing and praise through pain and disappointment. We believe and trust you. We pray according to your will that our joy may be full.

In Jesus Name, Amen.

Paul:
Never Give Up

"That is why we never give up. Though our bodies are
dying, our spirits are being renewed every day."
2 Corinthians 4:16

In Context

We have received the mercy and grace to live an
honest and true life before God and man. We don't
twist the Word of God. We speak truth before God.
The same gospel that saved you cannot be hidden
within you. It can't save lives that way. People who
embrace evil simply can't see the good news of
Jesus Christ and therefore don't believe. We must
share that Jesus is Lord and we are his servants. For
God who said, "Let there be light in the darkness,"
has made his light shine in our hearts – which are
like fragile clay jars containing a great treasure. This
makes it obvious our great power, is from God – not
ourselves. Life can be difficult, but this is how we
share in the suffering of Christ. But, we continue in
faith, confessing that, "We believe God," no matter
the circumstance. This is why we never give up. Our
troubles are here today, gone tomorrow. Instead we
look forward to a future we cannot see, a future that
lasts forever.

Simply a Vessel

If you consider any vessel, an item or object used for
the transportation of cargo from one destination to
another, as time passes it will become tattered and
torn. It is a natural progression. However, God has

created us as a unique type of vessel. The more his message and love travel through us, they also seep into us. They embed and become the very fabric of our souls. It's truth is passed down from generation to generation, with evidence of its blessings, protection and love earmarked in the history of time. As we experience unforeseen or unprovoked hardship, it is easier to look forward in hope because we know how the story ends. Keep sharing the good news that Jesus lives. Provide hope, healing and happiness for your neighbor, who may only see Christ through you.

"But he said to me, "My grace is sufficient for you, for my power is made perfect in weakness." Therefore I will boast all the more gladly about my weaknesses, so that Christ's power may rest on me."
2 Corinthians 12:9

In Context

Paul opens this chapter with, "I must go on boasting." Sharing the Word of Christ is what I was made to do. While I could brag about myself and everything I say would be true, I know that I am also weak. I have a constant reminder that I am weak, a message from Satan. I prayed and prayed for God to take it away from me, but he refused, sharing that in my weakness is HIS strength made perfect. For this reason, I boast all the more about my weakness, that Christ's power may rest on me. I delight in weakness, hardship and persecution. For when I am weak, I am strong. Please forgive me, I am returning to you (the church) and providing for myself. Sharing the gospel, I recognize that I may not be who you want me to be when I arrive. I am afraid that I may walk into a disarray of corruption and that God will humble me before you. I will also be full of grief.

Final Notes

Whether we are thrown into the fiery furnace by fault of others or self, God is strong enough and powerful enough to see us through. This fragile condition is a perfect environment to reflect the faithful and beautiful sovereignty of Jesus Christ. Don't fret, never give up on God or yourself. We fall down, but we get back up. Keep sharing the unfailing Word of God and by all means, keep believing.

PRAYER

Most Gracious and Heavenly Father,

Lord, thank you for being our rock. You are so wonderful, merciful, loving and faithful. As we continue to share the truth about your Word, help us to love ourselves and others. We see the thorns of others and those within ourselves and may get discouraged. Lift us up, Lord. Fill our hearts and minds with an abundant knowing and revelation of your presence. For your grace is sufficient. Forgive us when we fail. Our needs are being met. No weapon will prosper. You are restoring our souls. We are waiting for you Lord. We are expecting you Lord. We are praising you Lord! We delight ourselves in you, as you give us the desires of our hearts. We are more than conquerors through you. We can do all things through you. Lord, take our vessel and seep all of you into all of us. Decrease us and Increase your presence. Bless our families with knowledge and revelation of your presence, love, mercy and grace. We love you and we thank you.

In Jesus Name, Amen.

Hagar:
You Are the God Who Sees Me!

"Thereafter, Hagar used another name
to refer to the Lord, who had spoken to her.
She said, "You are the God who sees me."
She also said, "Have I truly seen the One who sees me?"
Genesis 16:13

In Context

Hagar was a slave to Sarah and Abraham. God gave Abraham a promise of having a son. Sarah did not believe she could bear a child, so she convinced Abraham to sleep with her servant, Hagar. But, as soon as Hagar became pregnant, the relationship between Hagar and Sarah became strained. Sarah was angry and upset with Abraham and Hagar. Abraham told her that it was not up to him what happened, but Sarah's decision. Sarah then treated Hagar so badly, that Hagar ran away. God found her by the well and began to speak with her. He promised her that she would give birth to a son whose name would be Ishmael, which means, "God hears," because the Lord has heard her cry of distress. God also shared that her son would be a fighter, at war with everyone – including his relatives. This is when Hagar, renamed the well, "The Living One Who Sees Me."

You Are Not Alone

Don't you just love talking to people who have a history with you? They know you, the environment, the foundational factors and they just seem to really understand what's going on, right? Imagine your garage door malfunctioning in a specific way. There are certain factors to consider and know about when trying to explain the problem to your repairman. To provide the right solution, you must articulate with efficient detail what the actual problem is. In this way, God has a unique clarity that places his super on your natural. You can trust that he will not only respond appropriately, but he is going to do exceedingly, abundantly more than you can ask, think, or imagine. If you trust him and seek him, he will provide, protect and prepare us for what comes next. God knows everything about us. There is nothing hidden or secret.

"But God told Abraham, "Do not be upset over the boy and your servant. Do whatever Sarah tells you, for Isaac is the son through whom your descendants will be counted. But I will also make a nation of the descendants of Hagar's son because he is your son, too."
Genesis 21:12-13

In Context

Sarah gives birth to Isaac (which means laughter), just as God promised. They were about to have a big celebration when Sarah sees Hagar and Ishmael making fun of Isaac. She is angered and demands they be sent away. Abraham is upset, but God says it will be ok. So, Abraham sent Hagar and Ishmael away. As their journey gets weary and they are all out of water, Hagar sets Ishmael by a bush and continues for about 100 feet. God hears the young man's cries as Hagar shares she cannot watch the boy die. God speaks to Hagar and reveals a well she didn't see. He promises her that Ishmael will be great and become a father of nations himself. The boy grew to become a successful archer and later married a woman from Egypt. Around the same time, Abraham enters into an agreement of mutual respect with Abimelech granting he and his family a safe life in the land of the Philistines.

Final Notes

God knows exactly where you are. He is on your side. He loves you and will always help you. Whether you are rejected or honored by men, God will see you through the journey of life with safe passage. He will not fail.

PRAYER

Most Gracious and Heavenly Father,

You are our refuge, our shield, our exceeding great reward. We are so thankful that you see and know us. Lord, on this day, we ask that you help us to hear you speak. We pray that we not only believe and trust what you say, but that we respond with obedient hearts. Lord, grant us supernatural favor on today, open doors no man can shut, give us wisdom seemingly beyond our capacity that is relevant and on-time. Lord, bless the work of our hands that we may bless others and let every word we utter on today bless those that hear it. Please forgive us of our sins and help us to be everything you have created us to be.

In Jesus Name, Amen.

Bathsheba:
How Shall We Be Saved?

She replied, "My lord, you made a vow before the Lord
your God when you said to me, 'Your son Solomon will
surely be the next king and will sit on my throne.'
I Kings 1:17

In Context

David was very old and about to pass. He was being
comfortable by the most beautiful woman in the
kingdom, Abishag. While his son, Adonijah decided to
host a banquet celebration declaring the kingdom
would soon be his. Nathan the prophet warned
Bathsheba, Solomon's mother, and instructed her
on how to inform the king. He too, would share the
distressing news. As soon as David became aware
of what was happening, he sprung into action. He
immediately called for Zadok the priest, Nathan
and Benaiah, son of Jehoida. He instructed them to
anoint, announce and blow the horn signifying that
Solomon was in fact, king over Israel and Judah. All
the people followed Solomon into Jerusalem, playing
flutes and shouting for joy. Adonijah and his guests
heard the horns just as they were finishing their
celebration. Adonijah asked for a report from a man
he trusted outside. The man declared Solomon was
king and that David praised God to see his successor
on the throne while he was still alive. His guests
scattered in fear as Adonijah ran to the temple,
grabbing the altar as he feared for his life. He plead,
"Let King Solomon swear he will not kill me!" Solomon
replied that the man's loyalty and agreeance to live in
peace would save him.

Fighting for You

God is always aware of what is going on. He will not allow your enemies to have the best of you. What is yours, is yours. Even while Solomon sat wondering what was going on, God had dispatched a solution and put it into play without his knowledge. Isn't wonderful to serve a God that fights for us? He knows, he cares and he lives. He is going to make sure that you are well protected – even when you can't see his protection.

> "And Adonijah the son of Haggith came to Bathsheba the mother of Solomon. And she said, "Do you come in peace?" And he said, "Peaceably."
> I Kings 2:13

In Context

As David clung to the last moments of life, he began to instruct Solomon on how to rule the kingdom. He told him to honor God that he may prosper in all that he does. He also instructed him on who to avenge and who to honor. David then passed away. Not soon after David's death, Adonijah approached Bathsheba, asking her to seek permission from Solomon to marry David's mistress, Abishag, the most beautiful woman in the kingdom. She promised to ask the king. As soon as Solomon heard the request, he became furious. He knew it was a ploy of Adonijah's to appear as though he was in the king's favor. Immediately, Solomon ordered his death.

Final Notes

We are snared in life by what we say and do. If Adonijah had simply stayed quiet, he could have lived a long peaceful life in the kingdom. But, his words (therefore his actions) came back to destroy him. Rather than accept his gift of life, he insisted on getting more and tried to use Bathsheba to obtain favor with Solomon. But Solomon saw right through him. God knows our hearts. He knows what is best for us. He spared Adonijah's life, only for Adonijah's actions to say, "It isn't enough. I want more." We must be careful to appreciate God's saving grace for every situation. Otherwise, how shall we be saved?

PRAYER
Most Gracious and Heavenly Father,

Thank you for being our Savior. Thank you for protecting us from dangers seen and unseen. Thank you for directing our path and making it straight. Lord, help us to be merciful and forgiving, giving others a second chance. Lord, also help us to be wise and discerning, recognizing when someone's intentions are not right. You are our rock. You are our shield. You are our exceeding great reward. You are a refuge. Allow us to rest beneath the shadow of your wings. Give us strength, without you we are nothing. Lord, on this day, we ask that you help us to honor you and keep your will and your way first. Lord, we also ask for open doors of divine favor, the anointing of your Holy Spirit, productivity that produces a fruit that shall remain, Lord, we ask that you teach us to be leaders. We know that humility must come first. Thank you for elevating us, for protecting our futures and for directing our steps. Forgive us of our sins. In the mighty and matchless name of Jesus we pray.

In Jesus Name, Amen.

Solomon: Above All, Get an Understanding

"Speak up for those who cannot speak for themselves,
for the rights of all who are destitute. Speak up and judge
fairly; defend the rights of the poor and needy."
Proverbs 31:8-9

In Context

Solomon shares a teaching King Lemuel's mother provided when he was a young man. It's basic premise and foundation is making wise choices, especially when finding a wife. She taught King Lemuel not to indulge in obsessive drinking, to be a voice for the voiceless, and to avoid women that would drain him of strength and vigor. Finally, she shares the value of finding the right woman. A woman that works hard and brings her husband peace and love. She can research a great investment and purchase it if desired. She opens her arms to the poor and has no fear when winter comes. She speaks with wisdom and faithful instruction is on her tongue. She keeps an eye on the bottom line and makes sure her family is taken care of. Her children and husband praise her. While a woman can be charming and beautiful, it is a woman that fears the Lord that is to be praised. Honor her for her hard work and praise her before the city.

Making Wise Choices

It is so important that we operate with wisdom, especially concerning the words of our mouth. The wisdom that King Lemeul's mother provided him taught him to not only choose a God-fearing wife, but to also praise her before the city. She taught him to be a voice for the voiceless. To recognize a noble woman is a woman that brings good and not harm. That a good wife will speak with wisdom and provide faithful instruction. When we hear a woman of God speak, we listen. When we see a woman of God work, we see diligence and excellence. When we hear a woman of God speak, we hear intelligence and thoughtfulness. While this teaching is primarily about women, much can be said for a man of God and the way he speaks. He is valiant, honorable, a defense and a provider. His words help to shape kingdoms and create long-lasting change (fruit that remains). A good man, a godly man, will not disrespect a woman in public or private.

"Wisdom is the principal thing; therefore get wisdom: and with all thy getting get understanding."
Proverbs 4:7

In Context

If there is anything you must obtain, let it be understanding. Wisdom will allow you to run without fear of falling. If you hear this, and believe it, and do it – you will live a good life. Wisdom will preserve you. It will bring you honor and promotion. Your wisdom will shine like a crown of glory. Stay away and out of the path of evil men. They can't sleep until they cause mischief and violence is a refreshing drink. But the path of the right man is bright and gets brighter every day. Don't speak evil or bad things, keep perverse sayings far from you. Consider where you go and let your way be established. Keep pushing onward.

Final Notes

The words we speak are containers of power. We can

be like the Proverbs woman, speaking wisdom and providing instruction. Or we can be like her husband, that praises her in the city gates. We can be like King Lemeul's mother, planting seeds of wisdom in our children that will bless many lives for years to come. Or we can be like the wise man that seeks understanding, is attentive to instruction and ready to hear a word from God. If we choose evil, we can destroy lives, companies, churches and more. We have the power to create or destroy with our words, consider what you say and be sure, so that your way will be established.

PRAYER

Most Gracious and Heavenly Father,

Thank you for the precious gift of wisdom. Thank you for mothers that care enough to share the important facts of life. Thank you for the opportunity to speak to you in prayer. Lord, as we consider our ways, help us to shine a bright light on what is good and to avoid what is evil. Grant us a supernatural wisdom and discernment to know who is for us and who is against us. Lord, help us to gain clarity and a greater understanding of our purpose. Help us to call those things that are not as though they already are. We are the lender and not the borrower, above and not beneath, the head and not the tail. No weapon formed against us shall prosper. Thank you for your provision, protection and direction. Thank you for blessing the words we speak, the actions we take, the people in our presence and our thoughts of purpose, destiny and your will.

In Jesus Name, Amen.

Noah:
The Grace to See
Another Day

"So the Lord said, "I will wipe from the face of the earth
the human race I have created—and with them the
animals, the birds and the creatures that move along the
ground—for I regret that I have made them." But Noah
found favor in the eyes of the Lord."
Genesis 6:7-8

In Context

The earth had become a place full of violence and
evil. The sons of God began to marry human women.
Their life span was reduced to 120 years. But still,
they were vagrantly disobedient and it upset God.
God vowed to flood the earth and destroy every living
thing that had breath. Noah, however, was a righteous
man and blameless. He found favor in the eyes of the
Lord. God gave him specific instructions on how to
build an ark. He told him to gather every kind of food
and pairs of every animal. Noah did exactly as God
instructed.

Favor in the Eyes of God

It is natural for humans to be evil. It is hard-wired
in our DNA. In order to be righteous, we must be
intentional, thoughtful and prayerful. Even then, we will
fall and make mistakes. No one is truly holy. But Noah
found favor in the eyes of God. The scripture calls him
righteous. Scripture also states that Moses believed
God and it was counted unto him as righteousness.

This can be attributed to faith. Faith believes what God says to be true. Noah believed God and did everything God told him to the letter and it not only saved his life but also the lives of those he loved.

"They will be called the Holy People, the Redeemed of the Lord; and you will be called Sought After, the City No Longer Deserted."
Isaiah 62:12

In Context

For the sake of Zion, God will not rest until you are vindicated. God is restoring it all. People won't talk about you the way they have been. Instead, they will call you what God calls you (blessed and highly favored of the Lord). You and your land will be married to the Lord; he will rejoice over you. You are a jewel in his crown. Keep praying, stay on task until God makes Jerusalem the praise of the earth. God will never give your increase to your enemies again. He will instead bless those that bless you and those that gather will eat grapes in his sanctuary. Rejoice, for your Savior is coming. He will redeem you and you will never be deserted again.

Final Notes

God is a redeemer of his people. When we show our faith by believing God's truth, his Word, we are blessed. Former hurt and pain is replaced with a Savior that never sleeps nor slumbers. A Savior that will marry you, find favor in you, and connect himself to you with gladness. He will see you as a jewel in his crown. The presence of Jesus in our lives not only gives us a reason to praise and thank God, but to see the blessing of another day full of grace, mercy and favor.

PRAYER

Most Gracious and Heavenly Father,

We appreciate your presence in our lives. You are faithful. You never change. Your forgiveness and love are everlasting, your grace and mercy abundant and pleasant. Thank you Lord for saving us from an evil pit, for rescuing us from the violence of our lives, for restoring everything the enemy tried to steal. Thank you. Lord, thank you for your mercy. We don't deserve your love, but we believe your promises and it has been counted unto us as righteousness. Thank you that we have found favor in your sight. Lord, as we walk on this journey, help us to be more like you each day. Open our eyes to see our actions and reactions. Open our hearts and minds to receive your word, and when we hear a message, let it be you and not us. Help us to number our days and be grateful for each one. Help us to seek you early, all day and all night. Help us to pray without ceasing. Help us to be a blessing and not a curse. Help us to bless others with your love, your message and your will. Forgive us of our sins and help us to be more like you each and every day. Allow us to decrease as you increase. Lord, thank you for all that you are. We give you glory, honor and praise.

In Jesus Name, Amen.

Abraham:
And He Believed God

"The Lord had said to Abram, "Go from your country, your
people and your father's household to the land I will show
you. I will make you into a great nation, and I will bless you;
I will make your name great, and you will be a blessing.
I will bless those who bless you, and whoever curses you
I will curse; and all peoples on earth will be blessed
through you."
Genesis 12:1-3

In Context

The Lord made a great promise to Abram. In
response, Abram believed God and left his homeland
as God instructed. He, his wife, and his nephew all
traveled to the land of Canaan. When they arrived,
God promised the land they were standing on to
Abram's descendants. When Abram heard this, he
built an altar. When he traveled to the other side of
the land, he called on the Lord and built another altar
there. However, there was a great famine in Canaan,
so they went to Egypt. As they entered Egypt, Abram
asked Sarai to pretend to be his sister. He thought
they would kill him and take her (because of her
beauty), if they knew she was his wife. The Egyptians
did favor Sarai and befriended Abram because of
it. He grew in stature and wealth until the Egyptians
began to recognize they were cursed because of
Sarai. Pharaoh called Abram and asked why he
would do such a thing and bring down a curse on him.
Pharaoh told him to take her and go, sending them
both on their way with all that Abram accumulated
during their stay.

Believing What God Says

There wasn't anything written with the promises God gave Abram. He simply heard God and believed God. His belief was so strong that when God said to go, he did. Abram did not hesitate to praise God by building altars of worship. He called on God. God also continued to speak to Abram. Abram's responsiveness to God was a sign to God that he trusted him.

"When Abram was ninety-nine years old, the Lord appeared to him and said, "I am God Almighty; walk before me faithfully and be blameless. Then I will make my covenant between me and you and will greatly increase your numbers." Abram fell facedown, and God said to him, "As for me, this is my covenant with you: You will be the father of many nations. No longer will you be called Abram; your name will be Abraham, for I have made you a father of many nations. I will make you very fruitful; I will make nations of you, and kings will come from you. I will establish my covenant as an everlasting covenant between me and you and your descendants after you for the generations to come, to be your God and the God of your descendants after you. The whole land of Canaan, where you now reside as a foreigner, I will give as an everlasting possession to you and your descendants after you; and I will be their God."
Genesis 17:1-8

In Context

God again affirmed his original promise to Abram, 24 years later. But this time, he changed his name to Abraham (father of many nations) signifying the promise was about to come into fruition. Then God began to give Abraham specific instruction for he, his descendants and his servants to abide by. If any chose not to abide, they would be broken from the promise. God also changed Abraham's wife's name from Sarai to Sarah and promised that nations and kings would come from her. Then God affirmed his promise again. Abraham laughed at the thought of he and his wife bearing a child in their old age. He immediately assumed the covenant was for his son, Ishmael, who was born to his wife's servant. But God clarified that he and Sarah would indeed have a son within the year. He also promised that Ishmael would bear a great nation as well. Again, Abraham believed God and did as God instructed.

Final Notes

This lesson is about our clear response to what God says. Often times our logic will tell us that one way is right, but when we listen and choose to believe God, miracles happen. Let's listen more clearly to hear what God is saying and respond with faith by doing exactly as he instructs.

PRAYER

Most Gracious and Heavenly Father,

Thank you for giving us the ability to hear you when you call. Lord, give us a mind and heart to obey, even when what you ask us to do may seem above and beyond what we think is possible. Lord, you are our shield and our exceeding great reward, help us to cherish the small moments we have to reach out to you with humility and eagerness. Lord, you are our guide through this life. Without your direction, we are lost. Lead us into your will and help us to praise you as we go along the journey. When we are in lean seasons, help us to remember that you are with us and that this too shall pass. Lord, thank you for blessing us with the power of your Word to speak over our lives and strengthen our faith. Please send your people so that we may operate in the body as one. Lord, help us to believe and do exactly as you instruct.

In Jesus Name, Amen.

The Ark
of the Covenant:
A Hedge of Protection

"The people all responded together, "We will do everything
the Lord has said." So Moses brought their answer back
to the Lord. The Lord said to Moses, "I am going to come
to you in a dense cloud, so that the people will hear me
speaking with you and will always put their trust in you."
Then Moses told the Lord what the people had said."
Exodus 19:8-9

In Context

The people were rescued from the slavery of
the Egyptians. Moses and the people were at Mt.
Sinai. Moses sought God on the mountain and God
answered him. He told him that if the people of Israel
obeyed his commands they would be a holy people
and a kingdom of priests. Moses told the people
what God said and they agreed to do God's will. Then
God told Moses he would speak to him before the
people so that they would always trust him. God told
Moses to make sure his people had clean clothing and
consecrated themselves before he returned in three
days. He told Moses to build a hedge of protection
around the base of the mountain so that the people
wouldn't get hurt when he arrived. So, Moses did
as God instructed. After three days, God returned
to speak to Moses. He descended as fire on top of
the mountain, which caused to react violently and
volcanically. There was a loud trumpet blast. Moses
went up the mountain to speak to God when God
instructed him to go and warn the people to keep

their distance. Moses reassured God that it would be ok because they built the hedge of protection as instructed. But God insisted, then he told Moses to get his brother Aaron, the priest. Moses went back down the mountain and warned the people again and got his brother Aaron.

A Hedge of Protection

Even though Moses did as God instructed and built the hedge of protection, God still told him to warn the people that if they got too close, they could die. The Ten Commandments, Aaron's rod and a container of manna rest in the Ark of the Covenant (also known as the Ark of Testimony). Those commandments are similar in that they serve as a hedge of protection for us as God's children. The wage of sin is death. We cannot change the consequence that comes with sin, but we can change whether we choose to sin. God says he always gives us a way of escape. In fact, God has given us the answers to the test... it is simply up to us to rest within it's protective hedge. Yes, Jesus defeated death and the grave, but we can live a peaceful life on earth if we learn to rest in the safe place God has created for us. Within the hedge of protection (The Ten Commandments) lies our own Garden of Eden.

"And God spoke all these words: "I am the Lord your God, who brought you out of Egypt, out of the land of slavery." Exodus 20:1-2

In Context

The Ten Commandments were given to Moses on Mount Sinai. God gave Moses the 10 ways we could be protected within his safety. He told Moses that we are to have no other Gods before him. That we were to make no idols and bow to them. That we were to never misuse the name of God. That we were to honor the Sabbath day and keep it holy. We were to honor our mother and father that we may have long life in the land the Lord give us. That we shall not murder, commit adultery, steal, bear false witness or covet our neighbor's blessings. When the people heard God speaking with Moses and heard the loud thunder and lightning, they were very afraid. They kept their distance and asked Moses to speak to God for them. Moses reassured them that this was just a test and way for God to show his power, but the people were afraid and stayed behind their hedge of protection. Afterward, God warned Moses to remind the people, "Don't create false idols." He shared with Moses how to create an altar where the people could worship God with sacrificial offerings. Then he promised, "Wherever I cause my name to be honored, I will come to you and bless you." Then he told him how not to make the altar or approach it.

Final Notes

God reminds us where we were (in slavery to sin) and where we could be without him. He offers us a hedge of protection that promises to bless us if we can stay within its boundaries. While we like the children of Israel may need to be warned several times, we can hear God and obey. With that promise, comes an abundant blessing. If we choose to ignore it, we could harm generations of our family for years to come.

PRAYER

Most Gracious and Heavenly Father,

Thank you for providing us with a hedge of protection. Lord, help us to stay within it's boundaries as much as possible. Help us to pray the way you have taught us to pray: Our Father in heaven, hallowed be your name, your kingdom come, your will be done, on earth as it is in heaven. Give us today our daily bread. And forgive us our debts, as we also have forgiven our debtors. And lead us not into temptation, but deliver us from the evil one.

In Jesus Name, Amen.

Father: Someone You Can Depend On

"Every good and perfect gift is from above, coming down from the Father of the heavenly lights, who does not change like shifting shadows."
James 1:17

In Context

When you are tested, count it all joy. For once you have been tested and survive, you will have life and more life. Don't point a finger at God accusing him of trying to make you sin, he would never do that. Instead, lust has a baby called sin and it is your choice, not an act of God. So, stay focused. All good things come from God, they are gifts that fall from the Father of light. Share this truth with everyone you know. But, don't allow this truth to flow through you without stopping to enjoy, understand and know what it really means. Then you will take action on what you hear in your spirit and show that you believe. Reach out to the homeless and loveless when they are at their worst and guard against corruption in a horrible world.

Doing Because You Believe

God is a faithful and loving God. He will never let you down. When hard times come or times of uncertainty arise, have faith. Listen for the Holy Spirit to guide you in all things. God is on your side and he is going to take care of you. Your actions will open doors of blessing, because through faith in God you are doing amazing things for others.

> "He who did not spare his own Son,
> but gave him up for us all—how will he not also,
> along with him, graciously give us all things?"
> Romans 8:32

In Context

There is nothing God won't do for us. He sent his son Jesus to save us. The most beautiful sacrifice sent to protect us in our most fragile and fractured human state. People who think they can live a full life without Jesus are fooling themselves. All they see is their ability, what they are able to do in life as opposed to the endless possibility and ability of God. If you know and trust God, you are listening to him, inviting him in. When God lives and breathes through you, you are no longer living a dead selfish life. Instead you are adventurously expectant, greeting God with a cheerful and curious spirit. God touches our lives and reveals our true relationship, God is our father and we are his children. When we let him in we can begin to see our purpose. We are more Christlike every day, and as we suffer with Christ, we celebrate with him as well. The difficulties we face are like childbirth, the pain is for a little while but the blessing is for a lifetime. All things are working together for our good, even when we don't understand. God does. He is praying for us when we don't know how to pray. He is completing the good work he has begun in us. Do you think anyone can drive a wedge between Christ and his love for us? No, nothing, absolutely nothing can stand between us and God's love for us.

Final Notes

I grew up without my father in the home. My parents

divorced when we were young. Years later, just as our relationship began to develop, a tragic circumstance ripped us apart. Unlike our earthly fathers, God does not have human limitations that can keep him from loving us and protecting us. His desire is to become one with us as Father and child. He is faithful and he will never, ever let us down.

PRAYER
Most Gracious and Heavenly Father,

Thank you for adopting us as your children. You have given us the ability to connect with you intimately, sharing our joy and our pain. You protect us from harm and comfort us through the worst of times. You see us through the most painful days of our lives. We thank you Lord. We thank you for sacrificing your Son, our Savior, Jesus Christ that you might save us and adopt us, so that we too can feel the love of the Father. Jesus said that you loved him before you formed the world. It is an immense and overflowing love that comes from the Father of lights. Thank you for that love Lord. Thank you for your presence. Thank you that we can communicate, spend time and know you a little bit better each day Lord. Thank you for your faithfulness in our lives. Thank you for the abundant life you have granted each of us. Thank you that no weapon formed against us shall prosper. Lord right now, we pray that you grant us wisdom and discernment. We want to be everything you have created us to be. Help us to shine in our purpose, becoming perfect conduits of your love, your mercy and your grace. Thank you for blessing us and keeping us despite our own struggles. Thank you that your grace is sufficient, for in our weakness is your strength made perfect. We celebrate you and honor you. We humbly bow before your throne of grace that we might find favor and mercy in the time of need. Move Lord, move in, over and through our hearts and minds that our hands may do the work you have assigned.

In Jesus Name, Amen.

The Son:
My Savior, My King

"So if the Son sets you free, you will be free indeed."
John 8:36

In Context

Jesus was teaching in the temple when the senior pastors brought him a woman caught having sex out of wedlock. They asked Jesus if the custom to stone her would be appropriate. Instead, Jesus kept writing in the sand beneath him without addressing them. They pressed him and pressed him. He responded, "The man that has never sinned may throw the first stone." Slowly, every person walked away. Then he asked the woman, "Where are they? Has anyone condemned you?" She responded, "No one, sir." Then he affirmed that neither would he and told her to leave her life of sin.

He began to teach that those who walk with him will never walk in darkness and will have the light of life. But the leaders in the church accused him of bearing false witness because he testified of himself. Jesus responded, "...My testimony is valid, because I know where I am going and where I have come from..."

Then Jesus shared that he was going where they could not come. He shared, "If you do not believe that I am He, you will indeed die in your sins." His statements made them question, "Who are you?" He told them that he has explained this from the beginning.

He then clarified the difference between a slave and a son. A slave to sin has no permanent place within the family, but a son belongs to it forever. So, if Jesus sets you free (from slavery), you are free indeed (family). Then he told them that their desire to kill him came from their true father (they believed Abraham/God was their father). But because they wanted to kill him when they heard him tell them the truth, Satan was their father. He only spoke what God told him to speak so their disbelief verified God nor Abraham was their father.

They accused Jesus of being possessed by a demon and thinking that he was greater than Abraham. Jesus assured them he would never give himself glory, but that glory belongs to the Father, and that it was God who glorified him. They picked up rocks to stone him, but he escaped.

Know Yourself & Believe

The religious leaders tried their best to tell Jesus he was wrong about himself. But, Jesus was confident in who he was, what his purpose was and where he came from. He knew himself and nothing they could say, would change that. Instead, he saved more lives, healed more people and continued to preach the Word of God.

"Jesus said, "Father, forgive them, for they do not know what they are doing." And they divided up his clothes by casting lots." Luke 23:34

In Context

They sentenced, crucified, murdered and buried Jesus. It began with accusations before Pilate, who finding nothing to charge Jesus with, sent him to Herod. Herod tortured Jesus, mocked him and returned him to Pilate. On this day, the two enemies (Herod and Pilate) became friends. Pilate, who found no guilt in Jesus, attempted to let him go. But the people chanted and chanted for Jesus to be crucified. It was so. Simon helped Jesus carry his cross. He was joined by two criminals, also scheduled to be crucified. One feared God and the other expected Jesus to save them all. The one who feared God was promised a place in paradise that day. The people watched as the leaders leered at Jesus on the cross. They mocked him and gave him vinegar to drink. Jesus stated, "Father forgive them, for they know not what they do." And soon, he was gone. The moment his life passed, the centurion spoke of his righteousness. Joseph, a mature and righteous man on the council, asked to prepare the body for burial, placing Jesus in a tomb never used. It was the day prior to the Sabbath, preparation day, and the women that followed Jesus saw him placed in his tomb. They went home to prepare the appropriate spices but rested on the Sabbath in obedience to the commandment.

Final Notes

The Lord is a loving, humble and caring man. After being accused, mocked and sentenced to death, he chose love over hate. Despite the community turning on him in a rage even inciting death, he asked God to forgive them. He understood that they were misled and misguided. Instead of getting angry, or getting even, or fighting back, he simply asked God to forgive them. It takes a strong person to forgive, especially while in the process of losing one's life. With a servant's heart, Jesus died that they might live forever. That we might live forever. He is our Savior, Our King.

PRAYER

Most Gracious and Heavenly Father,

Thank you Jesus for love, mercy and grace. We don't deserve to be forgiven for our sins, but you died that God might see your blood on the mercy seat when he looks at us. Your honor, your obedience, your love and your perfect nature has saved our lives in more ways than one. Thank you Lord for loving us and understanding us more than we love ourselves. Jesus, as we walk this earth, help us to be confident and understanding. Help us to be forgiving and merciful. Help us to be loving and bless others. Help us to show mercy when we would rather fight and defend ourselves. Help us Lord to have the strength to love. Please forgive us of our sins. Direct our path and make it straight. Help us to be more like you each and every day. We know that no weapon formed against us shall prosper and that vengeance is yours, you shall repay. Please help us to sow in love, forgive and show mercy.

In Jesus Name, Amen.

The Holy Spirit: My Comfort & Defense

"In the same way, the Spirit helps us in our weakness.
We do not know what we ought to pray for, but the Spirit
himself intercedes for us through wordless groans."
Romans 8:26

In Context

We are free from condemnation because Christ
paid the price for us all. If we are new in Christ, we
have our minds set on spiritual things, but if we are
focused on natural (fleshly) desires, we are led by
death. A mind governed by flesh is hostile to God.
But, if the Spirit of God lives within you, your body is
subject to death because of sin, but you are saved
from death because of the righteousness of Jesus.
We are adopted by Christ, and by him we cry, "Abba,
Father." We are co-heirs with Christ in that we share
in his sufferings and his glory. Our suffering does not
compare to the glory that will be revealed in us. We
hope and wait patiently. The Holy Spirit helps us in
our weakness. We don't know what to pray, but he
intercedes for us through wordless groans allowing
God to see our hearts. And we know that all things
work together for the good for those called according
to God's purpose. If God is for us, who could be
against us? If he gave us his son, why would he not
give us all things? It is God who justifies. As sheep sent
to the slaughter, we face death. But, we are more
than conquerors through him who loved us. Nothing
can keep us from the love of God.

He Knows Me

The Holy Spirit searches our hearts and brings a report back to God in groanings that we cannot hear or understand. In this, we know that God is fighting for us and protecting us, even when we can't see or feel it. We know because he promises that it is he who justifies. No matter how much we suffer, we are more than conquerors through Christ Jesus.

"At that very time He rejoiced greatly in the Holy Spirit, and said, "I praise You, O Father, Lord of heaven and earth, that You have hidden these things from the wise and intelligent and have revealed them to infants. Yes, Father, for this way was well-pleasing in Your sight."
Luke 10:21

In Context

Jesus sent 35 pairs of disciples into cities to preach the gospel. He shared that while the harvest is plenty the laborers are few and that they would be lambs amongst wolves. Then he told them that if they enter a home, speak peace over it and if they feel peace to stay. That they were to eat and drink as it was offered, and if they were refused or denied to shake the dust of that place off of them and move forward. He added that anyone that despises their teaching despises him and therefore God as well. The disciples returned with gladness telling stories of how even the devils were subject to them. But Jesus told them that while he gave them the power to tread on serpents and the enemy, they were to rejoice more over their names being written in heaven. He then thanked God for allowing him to share his gospel with those that are considered babes. He also shared that a man could not know God unless he was revealed to him by Jesus. Then in private he shared that the disciples were blessed to see what they were able to see and hear. After which, a lawyer challenged him on how a man could get into heaven. Above all, we are to love God with all that is in us and love our neighbors as ourselves. Jesus used the story of the good Samaritan to show how extending mercy to someone who isn't your friend or in your circle reflects loving another person as you would love yourself. Finally, Martha who was upset about Mary not helping her serve, asked Jesus if she should be helping her. Jesus shared with Martha that she was worried about so much, but instead there was only one thing she needed and Mary was doing the most important thing – learning more about him.

Final Notes

The Holy Spirit is the part of Jesus that is present with each of us at every moment. He is interceding on our behalf, protecting us and comforting us. He communes with Christ and allows God to see our hearts. He will not allow us to be condemned or defeated. While we may face opposition on every side, we have no reason to fear. We are more than conquerors through Christ Jesus. He has given us the power to tread on serpents and over all the power of the enemy and nothing by any means shall hurt us or separate us from God.

PRAYER
Most Gracious and Heavenly Father,

We are so appreciative for the power of the Holy Spirit that is at work within us. We do not deserve the wonderful and marvelous gifts of eternal life, forgiveness, mercy, protection and grace but we humbly and graciously receive them. Help us to live a life that honors you. Restore in us a clean heart and a right spirit that we may serve you in wholeness and truth. Grant us a supernatural spirit of discernment to see those that are for us and those that are against us. Grant us a wisdom that defies natural ability and catapults our ideas, strategies and applications of such into an area of unsurpassed elevation at the core of our family stability and increase, at the core of our business and opportunities, at the core of our ministry and healing and at the core of our friendships. God we are asking that you would bless us indeed and enlarge our coasts. We pray that your hand will be upon us and that you would keep us from evil that we may not be grieved. We thank you, we honor you and we praise you. We fully embrace and celebrate that God is love.

In Jesus Name, Amen.

The Last Shall Be First: Gratitude & Grace

"One of them, when he saw he was healed, came back, praising God in a loud voice. He threw himself at Jesus' feet and thanked him—and he was a Samaritan."
Luke 17:15-16

In Context

Jesus taught. Watch how you treat people, causing a child of God to sin can cause you great trouble. If someone sins against you, rebuke them. If they ask for forgiveness, forgive them (no matter how many times you travel through this cycle). If you have the faith of a mustard seed, you can make a tree obey you. A servant's duty is to be obedient. As Jesus traveled to a village, he was approached by a group of lepers begging for healing. He healed all 10 of them and they ran off with joy. But one of the men came back and praised God. He was a Samaritan. Jesus remarked, "Were not all ten cleansed? Where are the other nine? Has no one returned to give praise to God except this foreigner?" Then he said to him, "Rise and go; your faith has made you well." Jesus taught. The Kingdom of God will come like lightning. People will claim Jesus is here or there, but he won't be. People will continue to live life as though it is a party, but the day of reckoning will come quick, just as it did with Noah and the flood or Lot and the raining fire. When it is time to leave, don't look back at your life as though there is something for you. Consider Lot's wife... trying to keep your life will cause you to lose it. When Jesus arrives, of two, one will be taken. After Jesus spoke, his disciples asked, "Where will they go?" and his response was, "Where the dead are, the vultures will gather."

Surrounded by Vultures, Yet Grateful

People attack others all the time. They do mean things and desire to destroy them. Sometimes they repent, sometimes they don't. Either way, the Kingdom of God is coming. We are to forgive when asked, understand our responsibility, have faith, be grateful and be ready. The life we live now cannot be compared to the life we are receiving.

"He replied, "It is not right to take the children's bread and toss it to the dogs." "Yes it is, Lord," she said. "Even the dogs eat the crumbs that fall from their master's table."
Matthew 15:26-27

In Context

Jesus' disciples were accused of denying tradition because they didn't wash their hands before they ate. In return, Jesus challenged the religious leaders in their honor to the commandments. He explained to the crowd, "Listen and understand. What goes into someone's mouth does not defile them, but what comes out of their mouth, that is what defiles them." In this way, he explained that washing hands before a meal is not what makes a person foul. Later, he was approached by a woman whose daughter was possessed by a demon. Jesus responded that it was not right to give the dogs the children's bread. But the woman insisted that even a dog gets the crumbs from their master's table. He was impressed by her faith and healed her daughter. Later, he was healing many and a large crowd gathered. It had been three days and they had nothing to eat, and Jesus had compassion on them. His disciples only had a few small fish and couple loaves of bread. Jesus brake the bread, blessed the food and fed 4,000 that day. They picked up more than 7 baskets of leftovers. After, Jesus sent the crowd away and went to another city.

Final Notes

Listen and understand. God is teaching us how to win in life. Grace, gratitude, faith, forgiveness, responsibility, what we say and how we live are critical factors and God is paying attention. He is a loving and compassionate God. Jesus knows who we are, what we are experiencing, and he is on our side. We must learn to speak in alignment with what we believe.

PRAYER
Most Gracious and Heavenly Father,

Help us to listen and understand. Help us to seek you first when we make decisions that can affect not only our lives, but the lives of many others. Help us to believe that you are always for us and to have a stronger faith when things look bleak. Lord, you came that we might have life and have it more abundantly. Teach us your ways. For we desire and thirst for wisdom as only you give. Lord, direct our path and make it straight. Shine a light so that we may see the way that is best to go. Help us to hear your voice clearly. Lord, let the words of our mouth and the meditations of our hearts be acceptable and pleasing in your sight. Help us to forgive and Lord, please forgive us. Strengthen our resolve when we are attacked. Strengthen our backs when our burdens seem large. Help us to cast our cares upon you when they are too heavy to bear. Lord, we thank you for being a strong tower. We look to the hills, for where does our help come from? It comes from the

Lord. The Lord, mighty in battle. The Lord, our shield and our greatest reward. We thank you.

In Jesus Name, Amen.

In God's Strength:
A Mighty Warrior for God

"When the angel of the Lord appeared to Gideon, he said,
"The Lord is with you, mighty warrior."
Judges 6:12

In Context

Israel was in a tough place. After many victories, they found themselves back in sin and under the rule of the Midianites who stole everything they had. A young man named Gideon was hiding behind a wine-press threshing wheat when an angel of God approached him with a message. God told him that he would take down the Midianites as one man. Gideon couldn't help but be afraid. He didn't feel equipped. He didn't feel like he was able. He asked God for a sign to strengthen him.

In God's Strength

Gideon was alone minding his business when he was approached by God and given a heavy assignment. When he initially doubted God, the Lord turned to him and said, "Go in the strength you have and save Israel out of Midian's hand. Am I not sending you?" Signifying that when God places you on assignment, you no longer have to doubt. It doesn't matter how weak, or small you feel in your own eyes... he has strengthened you for the battle ahead.

"And let us not be weary in well doing, for in due season we shall reap if we faint not."
Galatians 6:9

In Context

The Message Bible opens this book with the following three words, "Live creatively, friends." It is the crux of operating based on faith. This book shares that we are to be humble and serve God's people. It teaches us to forgive, to help others, to chase our God given purpose, to understand that we reap what we sow, to be doers of the Word and it warns us not to be a dirty mirror (reflecting what is not real or true). Finally, we are to never give up on God.

Final Notes

God has placed many on assignment. We have permission to talk to God. To ask him for guidance, to share what is in our hearts, even if that message is full of fear and doubt. We have a God that understands us. Likewise, he has not left us alone to accomplish his will in our own strength, or in our own power. Instead, he has opened up the resources of heaven and allowed us to utilize our faith by becoming vessels that carry his love and protection to others. While, this assignment may come at the expense of suffering through ridicule, fear, abandonment and discouragement, we must walk forward in faith. It is by faith, that Moses saved the Israelites and brought them out of Egypt. It is by faith, that Rahab protected the men of God and saved her family. It is by faith, that Esther listened to her uncle Mordecai and saved God's people. It is by faith, that Joshua asked the sun to stand still that he might win his battle. Each of them, mighty warriors, risked their own lives to save the lives of others. It is by faith, that we have won many battles and saved the lives of those Christ has assigned to our charge. Our living is not in vain. In this way, we share our life with Jesus, operating within the body of Christ.

PRAYER

Most Gracious and Heavenly Father,

Lord God in Heaven, thank you for your most precious gift called faith (to believe in you, to call on you, to trust you). The battle is not ours, it belongs to you. While we are weak, you are strong. And we know that the effective, fervent prayer of a righteous man avails much. So, we call on you today Lord to strengthen us, to guide us, to remember us, to protect us and provide for us. We understand that obedience is love and as you call us to do mighty works, we respond with yes and amen. Thank you, for the joy of the Lord is our strength and no weapon formed against us shall prosper. The Lord is a strong tower, the righteous run in and they are saved. You are our hiding place, you will protect us from trouble and give us songs of deliverance. Lord we glorify you. We thank you. We humbly fall before your throne of mercy and grace. We cry, "Abba, Father," because you know our end in the beginning. You are the author and the finisher of our faith and we give you praise. We are blessed in the city, we are blessed in the field, we are blessed everywhere that we go.

In Jesus Name, Amen.

Opening Doors for You: Only One Holds the Key

"Thus says the LORD to Cyrus His anointed, Whom I have taken by the right hand, To subdue nations before him And to loose the loins of kings; To open doors before him so that gates will not be shut."
Isaiah 45:1

In Context

I God am sending a warrior. He doesn't even know me, yet I am sending him to terrify the kings that rule. I am going to kick down doors and barriers that he may enter without effort. That the world may recognize, there is no god that is able to stand against me. I created light and dark, good and evil. I am God, I work in the open, setting things right. So, turn to me, and be saved. I promise in my own name, every word out of my mouth does what it says. I never take back what I say. All who have raged against God will be brought before him, disgraced by their unbelief. All who are connected with Israel will have a robust, praising, good life in God!

He Holds the Key

God is God all by himself. Without help from anyone, he formed the earth and all within it. It is he that creates harmony and discord. It is he that has allowed every circumstance. It is he that will set you free. Kings will honor you because of the God within you, saying, "Amazing, God is with you!"

"I know your deeds. Behold, I have put before you an open door which no one can shut, because you have a little power, and have kept My word, and have not denied My name."
Revelations 3:8

In Context

In Revelations 3, a letter is written to each of the churches in Sardis, Philadelphia and Laodicea. To Sardis, God warns: I see you working but not for me. I know that you are busy but you are focused in the wrong direction. Return to what you heard originally and work in your purpose. You will not know when I am coming, repent. To Philadelphia, He assures: I open doors no man can open and shut doors no man can shut. I have seen you working hard to keep my word. Even when it was hard for you, you still believed. You have little strength, but you have held on. You have not denied my name. There are many that call themselves righteous but aren't being real. Hold on to your crown tightly and don't allow distractions to pull you away. When all is said and done, I will exalt you before them and all will know who really worshipped me in wholeness and truth. To Laodicea, God warns: Get it together. You teeter totter between good and evil but it would be much better if you make a choice to be one or the other. Trust me. I will make you white as snow and ensure that shame does not befall you. I am here because I love you and I want the best for you. Listen, I am standing at the door knocking. If you let me in, I will come in and eat with you. At my table, I sit among conquerors... Because only conquerors sit at the table in a place of honor. Just as I have conquered and sit at the side of my Father.

Final Notes

God has created all things. He is the ruler of all things. He opens doors no man can shut. He is a way maker and a burden bearer. In all things, we can give him praise, because all things work together for the good. God tells us that he prepares a table and at that table sits conquerors... those that were faithful in the most trying of times. Praise God because he will not allow you to be brought to shame and not one word that he utters shall fail.

PRAYER

Most Gracious and Heavenly Father,

Lord, we ask you for wisdom that you give to all freely without reproach. You are Lord of everything. Every knee shall bow before you. Every tongue shall confess, you are Lord of everything. Thank you Jesus for allowing us an opportunity to come before your throne of mercy and grace while we still have time. Lord, you promise that all of the words of your mouth are righteous, that there is nothing twisted or crooked in them and that they are straight to him who understands. We thank you. Thank you for saving us from ourselves. Thank you Lord for creating such a beautiful place for us to live in and beautiful experiences for us to know, understand and feel your unending love. Lord, help us to praise you every morning, every day and every evening. For you are worthy to be praised. For you have not given us a spirit of fear, but of power and love and of a sound mind. Forgive us of our sins. For you give great peace to those who love your law and nothing causes them to stumble. We thank you that you will not allow your servants to be brought to shame. You prepare a table before us in the presence of our enemies. You know what we stand in need of and you promise that you shall supply all of our needs according to your riches and glory in Christ Jesus. No weapon formed against us shall prosper. Help us to bless others with our words, thoughts and deeds. Help us to be perfect conduits of your message and your love. Lord, open doors no man can shut and close doors no man can open.

In Jesus Name, Amen.

Remember:
The Power of Life & Death

"So when he was raised from the dead, His disciples
remembered that He said this, and they believed the
scripture and the word which Jesus had spoken."
John 2:22

In Context

Jesus performed his first miracle of turning water
into wine at a wedding at his mother's request. She
told the young men to do whatever he tells them to
do. His disciples witness the miracle and believed.
Later, Jesus was in the temple. He saw men inside
the temple courts selling items for worship to false
gods. This made him extremely upset. He turned over
tables and waved them out of the temple. The Jews
asked him on what authority did he do all this? Then
Jesus responded, "Destroy this temple and I will raise
it in three days." He was referring to his body. His
disciples remembered this when he was raised from
the dead. Later that evening, at the Passover festival,
many saw him work wonders and believed. But Jesus
did not trust himself to them, because he knows the
heart of every man.

He Knows You

The power of life and death are in your tongue. We do
well to remember this in emotional times. The bride
and groom were probably in distress, hearing that the
wine was about to run out before celebration's end.
But Jesus' mother, in all her wisdom, told the young
men working the wedding to do everything Jesus told
them to do. She said this in faith, even after Jesus

told her it was not yet his time. We are to be like those servants, doing exactly what Jesus tells us to do. While the Lord had a special gift, his mother knew to value it and choose her actions wisely. We are better equipped when we do the same.

"Hope deferred makes a heart sick,
but a longing fulfilled is a tree of life."
Proverbs 13:12

In Context

Proverbs 13 shares a unique wisdom on the power of our words and actions. It shares that intelligence heeds its father's wisdom, but a mocker will not respond to rebukes. From the fruit of the lips, people enjoy good things, but the unfaithful have an appetite for violence. Guard your words and eat well, speak rashly and come to ruin. A sluggard wants more but a hard worker is satisfied. Good judgment wins favor – but the way of the unfaithful leads to destruction. Wise teaching avoids death. Poverty and disgrace come to him who ignores instruction. Misfortune pursues sinners. A wicked messenger falls into trouble but a trustworthy envoy brings healing.

Final Notes

The Holy Bible is a guide we can trust. When we accept Jesus as Our Lord and Savior, we become endowed with the Holy Spirit. Through the Holy Spirit we can communicate with God. We feel his presence and have a unique way of knowing what he expects and desires without reading it in the Bible. There is a revelation given to us for purpose, direction and protection. Alternatively, we can truly make a mess of things with what we say and do. Our words are containers of power that inspire action. That reaction can either be good or bad. If we only listen to God and do what he says (through the Holy Spirit and his Word), we will see the blessing. Wisdom is the application of knowledge.

PRAYER
Most Gracious and Heavenly Father,

Lord, help us to suture our lips, be still and be quiet when we should just listen and obey your instruction. Thank you for knowing us better than we know ourselves. Teach us in your Word. Help us to respond in obedience. Grant us a supernatural strength and wisdom to discern those that are for us and those that are against us. Remove any hindering spirits or persons in our circle and replace them with those that trust you and obey you. Help us to recognize those persons and to treat them with respect and honor. Help us to be humble before you. Release the anxiety in our hearts and increase our joy through your word. Lord, please forgive us of our sins and help us to be all that you have asked us to be. Bless our coming and our going and protect us from ourselves. We love you and praise you.

In Jesus Name, Amen.

Live:
We Walk By Faith

"For we walk by faith, not by sight."
2 Corinthians 5:7

In Context

As we wait within earthly bodies for our heavenly
calling, we can have faith. Our faith will remind us and
give us a hope to see what we believe. We will one day
live with Christ in heaven as he has redeemed us. He
is Our Savior and has given his body for ours. In this
we can have confidence. In Him, we live.

Confess Your Faith & Run

We can run with faith. Often, we allow our
circumstance to convince us of our outcomes. But,
if we only have a mustard seed of faith, we can walk
with confidence. We can possess an innate knowing
that what we believe in will come to pass.

"For I command you today to love the Lord your God,
to walk in obedience to him, and to keep his commands,
decrees and laws; then you will live and increase, and the
Lord your God will bless you in the land
you are entering to possess."
Deuteronomy 30:16

In Context

God says, come back to me. I am going to bring you out of that dark place and into your promised land. If you and your children love the Lord with all your heart and obey, all these blessings will come upon you – just like I promised your ancestors. God is going to make it possible to love him completely by performing a heart work in you and your children. He is going to avenge your enemies that hated you and tried to destroy you.

You will experience a brand-new beginning. If you listen and obey God he is going to outdo himself in blessing you. He will enjoy you again. But, only if you listen obediently to God and keep the commandments and regulations written in his Word. This requires complete submission to God and HIS way.

This is not too hard for you. Just do it. God is presenting an option: life or death.

Here is the warning: Do what God says when he says, serve HIM only – any deviance warrants death. You may get to the promised land but you won't stay long unless you obey.

Heaven as a witness, the choice is yours: life or death, blessing and curse. Choose life that it may be well for generations to come. Embrace God fully with an open heart and LOVE Him because he is life itself... settled on the land that he promised our ancestors long ago.

Final Notes

Our faith in God will dictate our actions. We can either choose life or death but it all comes down to whether we trust God or not. Undoubtedly, we will make mistakes. But after a while, God will restore us and bring us into a resting place with him. Faith comes by hearing and hearing the Word of God. If we are faithful to confess what we believe and know about God we are destined to grow in faith. If we walk by faith, we will choose life, speak life and enjoy life flourishing in the land the Lord promises to give us. Have faith, don't faint, God is not slow in keeping his promises toward us. He is an on-time God. He is faithful.

PRAYER
Most Gracious and Heavenly Father,

You know us. Our hearts, our hands, our thoughts... our being, nothing is hid from you. You knit us together perfectly within the wombs of our mothers, nurtured us in our youth and protected us as we stumbled into adulthood. Lord, you know us. In this life, many things have hindered the way we see ourselves. Help us to see ourselves as you see us. Strengthen our faith. Hold us up when we feel faint. Breathe air into our collapsing lungs that bear the whispers of failure, defeat and despair. Give us confidence and faith. Help us to remember that we are more than conquerors through Christ. Help us to remember the days of old, when you rescued us from our enemies and our own mistakes. Help us to stand on your Word of faithfulness, believing, confessing and trusting you with our lives. Lord, help us to answer, yes, when you call. Help us to have an unwavering walk on water faith to run when you reveal our purpose, to speak when we know you call us and to live according to your will. We love you and thank you on this day, a day you have allowed us to live and breathe with new mercy and grace.

In Jesus Name, Amen.

Salvation: All Things are Possible with God

"When the disciples heard this, they were greatly astonished and asked, "Who then can be saved?" Jesus looked at them and said, "With man this is impossible, but with God all things are possible."
Matthew 19:25-26

In Context

Jesus was healing when approached by religious leaders. They asked if a man could divorce his wife for any reason. Jesus responded that no man should divorce unless there is sexual immorality. He also stated that some were created to be eunuchs or became eunuchs and that if it was possible for them to live that life, it was good. Then parents wanted to bring their children to be blessed by Jesus, but his disciples refused. Jesus insisted that they bring the children for the kingdom of heaven belongs to them. Then a rich man asked, how could he get into heaven. Jesus told him that if he wanted to be perfect, to give all his possessions to the poor and he would have riches in heaven. The man walked away sad. Then his disciples asked how a man could be saved if this was the case. Jesus responded, "With man it is impossible but with God all things are possible." Then Peter asked about his end, being that he'd given up all to follow Jesus. Jesus then shared that the disciples would sit on twelve thrones to judge Israel. However, a man that walked away from his life to follow a life of God would be blessed in heaven one hundred fold.

All Things are Possible with God

Life is beautiful. Love, marriage, children, friendships and business encourage us to wake up daily, refreshed and ready to take on a world of adventure and happiness. But, as we begin to follow Jesus and pursue the purpose he has for us, some of those things can fall away, dissipate and eventually leave you alone with God and your purpose. It can be difficult to follow God in these moments. Because even as you pursue purpose with God, we fall under attack. We get lonely. We get frustrated. We get weak. While fulfilling purpose is a good thing, you must be strong and solely dependent on God to walk it out. The life of a eunuch isn't for everyone, but if it is possible for you to walk it out, it is good.

"Salvation is found in no one else,
for there is no other name under heaven given to mankind
by which we must be saved."
Acts 4:12

In Context

Peter and John were preaching the Gospel of Jesus Christ and healed an older man. The people praised God in heaven and began to believe in great number. The religious leaders took John and Peter captive and asked by what name and power they spoke. The men asked if they should be questioned for doing a good deed in healing the man. Peter, filled with the Holy Spirit, shared that it was by the name of Jesus Christ, whom they rejected but God rose from the dead that they preached. The religious leaders dismissed them to discuss in private. They called them back in and insisted they stop preaching in the name of Jesus Christ. But, Peter and John asked if it was better to obey them or God. In this the religious leaders dismissed them but were frustrated. Upon release, the two men went directly to fellowship with other believers. They all began to pray to God. They praised God and asked why do the rulers plot in vain and stand against Jesus and those he anointed to do his work. They prayed that the servants of God would speak his Word with boldness. They also asked God to stretch his hand that they may serve and perform miracles through the name of Jesus. After their prayer, the building shook and they spoke the word of God boldly, being filled with the Holy Spirit. After this, they were one in heart and mind, sharing their possessions – even selling their possessions to further the spread of the Gospel of Jesus Christ. No one was in need.

Final Notes

Confession is good for the soul and prayer brings peace in all situations. But, salvation will come through no one else. There is one name under heaven by which all men can be saved, and that is through the name of Jesus Christ. We can seem to live a life of lavishness, beautiful cars, houses and possessions, picture-perfect families and business' that flourish, but without God at the helm, we are nothing. We must confess, know and believe beyond any doubt that Jesus is Lord. If we trust God and are able, we can commit our lives to him. As we walk in our purpose, we will lack nothing but gain all.

PRAYER

Most Gracious and Heavenly Father,

What does it profit a man to gain the whole world but lose his soul? Is our living in vain? We commit our work to you, that our plans may be established. We trust you. We speak the Word of God that our faith and the faith of others may be strengthened. Thank you for the perfect gift of salvation. As we are careful to serve you not only in what we say, but also with what we do, help us to see your will in it all. Lord, protect us from those that seek to destroy us as we walk in your purpose. Forgive us for falling short of the glory of God. Direct our path and make it straight, that we might serve you in truth. Lord, as we embark on the adventure of a lifetime, keep us strong, keep us in faith, keep us in the palm of your hand. Strengthen us for the battles that may come and provide our needs as we continue in your grace. No weapon formed against us shall prosper and every tongue that rises against us in condemnation, you shall condemn for this is the heritance of the servants of the Lord, and our righteousness comes from you. We speak boldly in your name and we believe that all things are possible with God. Help us to live a life that reflects the Living Proof, the almighty, I AM, our Savior, Jesus Christ. We give you praise, we give you glory, we give you honor.

In Jesus Name, Amen

THE LIVING PROOF

"Kind words are like honey—
sweet to the soul and healthy for the body.."
Psalm 16:24

We can easily quote our favorite musicans, storytellers, artists or greats like Martin Luther King, Jr. or Maya Angelou because the power and strength of our words echo. We remember the words of those that hurt us in our youth because their words haunt us. God's Word was provided that we might be led in the way of truth. His Word is a light to our path and it heals us. It strengthens our faith and provides wisdom. When we intentionally speak God's Word over our lives, we release the power of God and allow it to work in our lives and the lives of those we love and care for. Let's encourage ourself and others. We are what we say. Let's begin to speak life!

ECHOES
Tried, Worn Out & Over It
Ignoring the Echoes & Listening to God's Voice
by stephanie d. moore

31-Day Devotional
HIS favor
stephanie d.
It's not about obtaining HIS favor...
It's about recognizing you already have it!

Living
ON PAPER
Praise, Epic Poetry
and Sonnets for the Sultry Soul
by stephanie d. moore

NOTHING IS BIGGER THAN OUR GOD!
OBEY
obedience breaks every yoke
by stephanie d. moore
31 Day Devotional Divine Leadership

31-Day Devotional
INTO THE
Promised Land
by stephanie d. moore
Desperately Seeking the PRESENCE OF GOD
in the Wilderness on Your Journey
INTO THE PROMISED LAND!

BETRAYED
FAMILY SECRETS
by stephanie d. moore

31 DAY DEVOTIONAL
And God is able to make all grace abound to you,
so that always having all sufficiency in everything,
you may have an abundance for every good deed.
2 Corinthians 9:8
ABUNDANCE
Faith & Wisdom
MOVING YOUR MOUNTAIN
by stephanie d. moore

God is faithful!
blush
you are the apple of my eye
A 31-DAY DEVOTIONAL
OF GOD'S UNENDING LOVE FOR YOU
stephanie d. moore

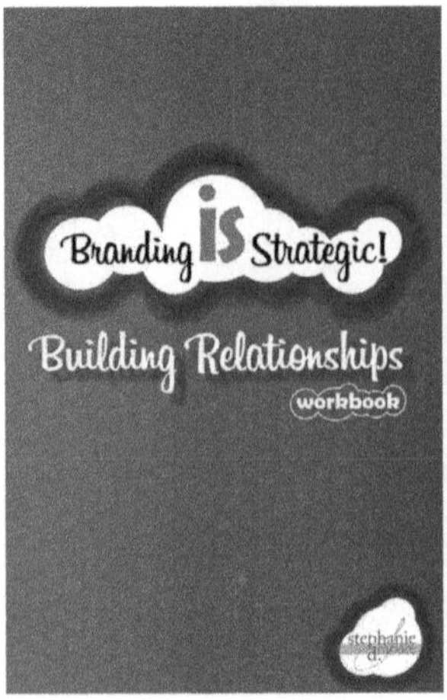

Branding IS Strategic!
Building Relationships
workbook
stephanie d.

About the Author

Stephanie D. Moore

Stephanie D. Moore was born in Muskogee, Oklahoma. She graduated from Putnam City North High School in 1994. She was married in February of 1996. She is the mother of 3 beautiful daughters, and has a grandson. She graduated with her Associates in Technology, and a Bachelors in Communications. She holds several design and technology certifications and has won numerous awards in that area. Stephanie has worked in television, print and web media for more than 15 years.

An Author with a Heart Full of Passion

At the age of 9, I was molested by a friend of her family. In high school, I held the hand of a friend as he died from a fatal gun shot wound... despite prayers for God to save him. As an adult, I was the victim of a violent acquaintance rape. Subsequently, I struggled with personal demons. But when I sought the Lord and his Word, my life was forever changed. I Give God ALL the Glory! He is and will always be the head of my life. He is my joy, my strength, my everything. My constant prayer is to be a perfect conduit of his message and love.

Owner of Moore Marketing and Communications. Her company serves in the following areas: strategic marketing plans, public relations, writing, print and web design. Stephanie has also served as a political consultant for Governor, Lt. Governor, State Representative, Mayoral and City Council candidates.

She's a
BOSSE

Stephanie has created and sponsored teen etiquette and leadership programs for young ladies and young men. The program for young ladies is called, She's a BOSSE (A Beautiful Oasis of Success, Style and Elegance) and the young man's program is called Grindaholix: Young Men on the Rise.

GRINDAHOLIX

MooreToRead.com   StephanieDMoore.com